LIFE, RECONSTRUCTED

A WIDOW'S GUIDE TO COPING WITH GRIEF, FINDING HAPPINESS AGAIN, AND REBUILDING YOUR LIFE

TERESA AMARAL BESHWATE, MPH

LIFE, RECONSTRUCTED

Disclaimer

Life, Reconstructed is sold with the understanding that neither the publisher nor the author is engaged to render any type of psychological, legal or any other kind of professional advice. The content is the sole expression and opinion of its author. No warranties or guarantees are expressed or implied by the content herein.

Neither the publisher nor the author shall be liable for any physical, psychological, emotional, financial, or commercial damages, including, but not limited to, special, incidental, consequential, or other damages. You are responsible for your own choices, actions and results.

If you find that the suggestions in this book do not help your state of mind, health or well-being, you are urged to seek the care of a physician or mental health professional. Do not delay if you find yourself in a state of depression or other condition that keeps you from functioning. If you are having thoughts of ending your life, please call 800-273-8255.

ISBN: 978-0-578-31154-8

LCCN: 2021921258

This book is dedicated to Ted, who taught me what it's like to be adored and who correctly predicted that I would write a book someday.

CONTENTS

Acknowledgments	9
What people are saying about Life, Reconstructed and Coach Teresa Beshwate	11
Get the Support You Need, For Free	15
Foreword	17
Introduction	19
Fundamentals	23
1. The "Right" Way to Grieve	25
2. Your Brain on Grief	28
3. The 50/50 Mix of Emotions	31
4. Why Can't I Stop Overeating, Overdrinking, Overspending, or Binge-watching?	34
5. Facts Are Different Than Thoughts	38
6. Thoughts Create Feelings	40
7. Feelings Prompt Action or Inaction	43
8. Actions Become Results	45
9. Pain versus Suffering	47
The Past	51
10. Power Over the Past	52
11. Got Guilt?	55
12. Wrestling with Reality	58
13. Why You Don't Have to Let Him Go	61
14. Why You Don't Have to "Move On"	64
15. Finding Freedom in Forgiveness	66
16. Beliefs, on Purpose	70
The Present	75
17. The Fear Factor	76
18. Is Familiar Discomfort Holding You Back?	79
19. Scarcity or Abundance?	83
20. Why Negative Is Natural	86
21. Overcoming Overwhelm	89
22. Decision Fatigue	92
23. Emotional Courage	95

24. Bridges and Ladders to New Thinking 98
25. Identity Crisis 101
26. Three Steps to Finding Yourself 104
27. Extreme Exhaustion 108
28. Alone but Not Lonely 111
29. Envy, Widowed Style 115
30. How Gratitude Can Stall Healing 117
31. He Would Be So Disappointed in Me 120
32. Celebrating Widow Wins 123
33. When and How to Deal With His Things 126
34. The Manual: Part 1 130
35. The Manual: Part 2 133
36. Boundaries: What They Really Are 136
37. Fear of Being Judged 139
38. A Simple Approach to Reducing Mental Clutter 142
39. Creating Confidence 146
40. Why You Can't Stop Hitting the "Escape Button" 149
41. The Best-Kept Secret to Achieving What You Want (Allowing Urges) 153
42. Belief Plan for the Present 156
Looking Ahead 161
43. What Moving Forward Doesn't Mean 162
44. What Will People Think? 165
45. "Cheating On" Your Late Spouse 168
46. Dare to Dream 171
47. Dear Newly Widowed Self 174
48. Bumping into Limiting Beliefs 177
49. Failing Forward 181
50. Added Capacity for Love 184
51. Generating Any Feeling 187
52. How to Create Any Result 190
53. Identity Creation 194
54. Moving Forward Confidently 197
55. Post-Traumatic Growth 200
56. A Belief Plan for the Future 203
Special Occasions 205
57. Planning and Navigating Birthdays, Holidays, and Other Special Occasions 206
58. An Authentic Christmas After Loss 209
59. The New Year's Eve Thought That Changed Everything 212

60. Anniversaries 214
Epilogue 217

Resources 219
Sources Cited 221

ACKNOWLEDGMENTS

This book is thanks to many people who constitute "Team Teresa" and for whom I am so very grateful.

To my parents and brother who chartered a plane to get to me on the day of my loss and have since gone the extra mile to be my unfailing source of support and encouragement.

To my family and my Beshwate family who have loved me unconditionally and supported me every step of the way.

To Kathleen for being by my side on my darkest day.

To my dear friend Erma whose wisdom and gentle guidance helped me through my first year. To my friend Pete who would regularly scoop me up into a bear hug and order me to keep going, no matter how tough it was. To Harmony who has been by my side for more than three decades. And to countless other friends who have loved and prayed for me day in and day out.

To my neighbors who have never stopped showing up at a moment's notice when I needed them, including those who act anonymously (I know who you are).

To Roger Landry, Larry Landry and my Masterpiece family. Every grieving person should know the love and support you have shown me.

To the perfect strangers in Carson City, Nevada who wrapped their arms around me on the day of my loss. Because of you, I know what it's like to feel the love of strangers and always aim to pay that forward.

To my clients for trusting me with their journey. I adore you, I believe in you and I celebrate you.

To The Life Coach School and founder Brooke Castillo, whose coaching tools and concepts are shared throughout this book.

And to Sonny, a man who can fix anything but never tried to fix me. The greatest gift is to be accurately seen, accepted and kept company in exactly that place. Thank you for walking patiently by my side as I figured out how to live again, for your calm and confident presence in my life, and for showing me that it's possible to have new capacity for love.

WHAT PEOPLE ARE SAYING ABOUT LIFE, RECONSTRUCTED AND COACH TERESA BESHWATE

Life, Reconstructed has shed a brilliant light on the path she has so expertly navigated.

Roger Landry, MD MPH, Author of *Live Long, Die Short: A Guide to Authentic Health and Successful Aging*

Life, Reconstructed is full of practical advice for normalizing the widowed journey, tools and techniques to rebuild a sense of self, and fundamentals that aid in understanding that *our own unique way* is the right way to grieve the loss of our spouse. The pages of this book are generously packed with practical recommendations, chapter summaries and real-life applications for everyone attempting to rebuild, recreate and restructure a life after the death of a spouse. Teresa, thank you for this book. *Life, Reconstructed* will help millions!

Susan Hannifin-MacNab, MSW, widowed 9 years
Author of *A to Z Healing Toolbox: A Practical Guide for Navigating Grief and Trauma with Intention*

Who better to coach another widow than a widow herself? This book is a MUST-READ MUST-DO guide for building a new life...moving forward without your spouse. Masterfully written and superbly relevant.

Kathleen M Townsend, RN,C, widowed 1 year

I have spent the last 35 years of my life ministering to thousands of people in grief, and I will use this resource in the work that I do. Life, Reconstructed is a wonderful journey through the grief process that offers concise and practical information to help someone process the loss of a spouse. Teresa's approach can truly help us move forward.

Craig Francis Harrison, grief expert

Before I met Teresa, I was just getting by. I felt lost and empty with no real direction or purpose. The most difficult part was that I was afraid that I would never feel better again.

My biggest insight during our coaching has been that I get to choose my thoughts, and I get to choose whether I suffer: because pain and suffering are not the same. Who knew?

Life, Reconstructed makes sense of the trauma and confusion that is a widow's shattered life. With compassion and guidance, I gained the tools and confidence I needed to work through the pain. I found Life, Reconstructed to be a Godsend.

Lora Bailey, widowed 2 years

When I read Life, Reconstructed, I knew I had found my reference guide for life after loss. It's like Teresa is in the room speaking directly to me. When I struggle with feelings, I can quickly find the chapter I need, reread it, and instantly feel like she's coaching me through the tough spot.

Before I started coaching with Teresa, I was paralyzed in my grief process, isolated and overwhelmed. How would I survive financially, emotionally, and spiritually?

Working with Teresa has given me clarity, a sense of calm, and decimated my anxiety levels! I'd recommend coaching with Teresa to people who want to integrate their past with their present, and take brave steps into a future that could be equally fulfilling and meaningful.

Julie Martella, widowed 4 years

Teresa helped me see that the feelings I was having were very normal and part of my journey.

But, with Teresa's coaching I was able to get out and actually heal. I love her!

If I had continued down the path I was on I would have been stuck in grief and not able to enjoy the blessings that were in front of me. I would have been very sad, probably negative, and lonely.

I learned that I am normal and that I am a different person today than I was prior to losing my husband. I also learned that my thoughts were generating feelings and that my primitive brain was keeping me safe from risk and loving again. I learned what I really wanted and needed and how to move forward with grief. Not through it or around it but with it.

Theresa Bolin, widowed 2 years
(and has now found her prince)

Teresa has taken me from undoubtedly the worst time of my life after the loss of my husband to a place of reassurance and hope for the days ahead.

Teresa has become a trusted confidante because I know that she REALLY understands every thought I have. She's been right where I am. She gets it.

I'm so grateful that I've found Teresa Beshwate and her profound work on helping widows travel through the pain of loss and recovery. Her program and book will have a lasting effect on me for the rest of my life.

Nancy Lacey, widowed 1 year

For those who want to ease their pain and build a new life after devastating loss, Teresa truly has a gift for this work. She is insightful and intuitive, and gently leads the way.

Before I started coaching with Teresa, I was consumed with grief for my dear husband and had a despairing view of a future without him. I felt so lost and powerless, utterly unmoored.

Now I no longer have to endure the suffering that I had been experiencing along with the pure pain of losing my beloved. Now I have tools to guide me as I move forward, with him ever-present in my heart.

Life, Reconstructed reads like a "hiker's guide", directing you along the path of grief towards a new life. It provides the most effective tools to use as you need them. If you are looking for a manual on rebuilding your life after devastating loss, read Life, Reconstructed. It will show you the way.

Catherine Presler, widowed 2 years

For more impact stories,
go to www.thesuddenwidowcoach.com/impactstories

GET THE SUPPORT YOU NEED, FOR FREE

Reading the concepts in this book is a start, but actually *applying* them to your life is where the transformation truly begins. Go to www.thesuddenwidowcoach.com/lrbook for additional free resources to take more efficient steps forward in your journey, starting today. My gifts to you include:

The Life, Reconstructed Downloadable Workbook

Putting pen to paper is powerful. This free workbook will help you consider the concepts in this book and apply them to your life right now. You will understand your journey better, be "on to" your brain like never before, gain new insights, and explore new possibilities.

Downloadable book club discussion questions

There is power in community, and it is my hope that this book brings people together, facilitates meaningful conversation, sparks new ideas and creates lasting friendships. This free resource provides questions that initiate conversation and create connection.

Ask the Author: Are you needing clarification or wanting more insight? Ask the Author is your chance to interact with Teresa.

FOREWORD

Gene Fowler said, "Writing is easy. All you do is stare at a blank sheet of paper until drops of blood form on your forehead." Teresa Beshwate has done that for the widows who are treading the trail she herself has walked for the last nine years. This gut-wrenching, *Life, Reconstructed,* exudes empathy and compassion on every page. Tears most certainly have marked many pages of this manuscript…I know that for a fact.

Teresa has been a colleague of mine for nearly fifteen years. Ted, her husband, a friend and fellow Vietnam veteran was a bigger-than-life presence, wherever he was. His passing left a hole in the world, which, in time, I came to terms with. Observing Teresa, however, even from three thousand miles away, was a difficult, heart-rendering long process. A process that I confess, despite losses in my own life, left me feeling powerless, uncertain and confused…until now.

Life, Reconstructed has shed a brilliant light on the path she has so expertly navigated. For me, I now understand the things she couldn't then articulate. I now know where I helped, or at least didn't hurt, and where I did indeed fall short. But for those who find themselves on the same road she traveled, this work is so much more: a colossal gift of comfort, understanding, and yes, love. But more than compassion, it is the parting of a dark sea… it is a hand to hold as a widow encounters the odyssey of fundamental loss.

Teresa was a coach before she was a widow, and that, I believe, has made all the difference. She was not a trained life coach as she is now, but her work with older adults to empower them to a healthy longevity helped hundreds enjoy the third chapter of their lives. Many of these older adults were widows…an unexpected training ground. Those years of experience, along with her degree in Public Health and the no-nonsense approach of a horse woman, when poured into the cauldron of her sudden, crushing loss, yielded a metaphorical salve of understanding for the deepest of wounds.

This book is for widows. This book is for widowers, for people with PTSD, for anyone experiencing a major loss. This book is for those who are trying their best to support their loved ones through these losses. This book is a celebration of what it is to be human, with all the ups and downs that go with it. This book is a tribute to Teresa Beshwate… and to Ted, and to all the Teresas and Teds out there and to come. I only wish I had the wisdom in this book with me when I was awkwardly attempting to comfort the widows of my patients and military comrades.

Teresa Beshwate has drilled down into the depths of her soul in order to help others… truly as unselfish as any human can be. She is indeed, a "candle for your darkness."

Roger Landry MD MPH, Cape Cod, MA

INTRODUCTION

My husband Ted always said that I would write a book. I rejected this notion because, given all the books ever published, I figured that I didn't have anything unique to offer. We agreed on most things, except this.

We met in 1999 and in September of 2000 began a marriage that can be described as peaceful, respectful, loving, hilarious, and an example of what is possible for a married couple.

Our wedding anniversaries were special to us, and each year we would celebrate with a trip. Sometimes we stayed close to home, and twice we traveled to Portugal and walked the cobblestone streets of the villages from which my family emigrated.

We were out of state celebrating our twelfth anniversary and having lunch when Ted's heart stopped beating. I did CPR, the paramedics arrived quickly, and the emergency department worked tirelessly. But in the quiet room of that hospital I heard the words "He died," and my life was instantly divided into two parts: before and after.

I found myself in two funeral homes in two states in a matter of two days. On our wedding anniversary I picked a casket. It felt so cruel at the time.

I couldn't eat or sleep. I was willing my heart to beat. The weight on my chest was preventing my lungs from drawing a deep breath. My body was on a slow march toward joining him. I realized that broken heart syndrome isn't suicide; it's the inability to fight dying.

In the days and weeks after losing Ted, I had two questions: Could I live? And even if I could, did I want to? I couldn't seem to find answers to those questions until, months later, I remembered the look on my mother-in-law's face at her son's funeral. I couldn't do that to my parents. So I decided to dig my heels in and fight my own dying. I had found my first *why*.

When I was cognitively able to go back to work, I jumped in with both feet. I remember the first day I was able to stay focused at work for eight straight hours. Those hours were like a vacation from my shattered life. That day I found my drug of choice—busy—and I was instantly hooked.

My full-time job at the time required significant travel, and I was adamant about continuing to live on our ten acres, so there was plenty to do to try to escape the horrific pain. I was on the run. I was exhausted physically and mentally, and the exhaustion reached the depths of my soul, yet I couldn't face the pain. Instead, I chose to be busy. I thought if I stayed busy long enough, maybe time would heal.

Years later it became obvious that my strategy wasn't working. Time on its own, I learned, does not heal. I was tired to my core, and tired of being tired. I was tired of grief beating me up every time I let my guard down. My strategy of avoidance was not getting me to where I wanted to go.

With a few exceptions, my journey was a solo one. I quickly realized that most people in my life, despite wonderful intentions, just didn't get it. Unless you know, you don't know.

While for many people therapy is a wonderful path to healing, it wasn't a fit for me. I felt that unless the therapist herself was widowed, no matter how educated and experienced she was, her advice wouldn't seem relevant to me.

Grief groups also weren't a fit for me. Grief felt like a private matter.

I stumbled around in the darkness until I started to see a light. No one ever told me that navigating great loss is nothing more than a series of decisions. I didn't know that my preconceived notions about right and wrong were holding me hostage. I had no idea that my thoughts were 100% optional, sometimes completely untrue, and often creating unnecessary suffering.

I didn't know how to feel such intense, soul-shattering pain. I was shocked to learn that when I turned and faced it, the pain did not overwhelm me but instead actually loosened its grip.

I had no idea that it was possible to find my way forward without leaving him behind.

I could have never imagined that our twelfth wedding anniversary—the day that I selected my husband's casket—would become my measuring stick for all other days. The torture of that day became my superpower.

Everything I didn't know when I was stumbling around in the darkness can be summed up in just two words: coaching tools. If only I had discovered life coaching sooner, my journey would have been much clearer, more focused, less confusing and more intentional.

So, I became a certified life coach so I can help you navigate your loss with clarity, focus and intentionality. I want to help you find your superpower. Let's begin.

....

This book contains chapters that stand alone and can be used for reference. The book can also be read cover to cover. At the end of each chapter, I offer ideas for application, such as journal prompts, questions, and tips. These applications will support you if you read the book solo and if you use it with a group.

The following section, "Fundamentals," is a must-read-first, then, feel free to read any other section or chapter in any order. The "Special Occasions" section is meant to support you as holidays, birthdays, and anniversaries approach.

....

There is hope. There is a way through. Let this book represent a candle in your darkness.

FUNDAMENTALS

In order to fully understand this book's other chapters, you'll need to start here. I want you to know the most important things that no one told me early in my journey—the things that would have helped me to understand myself better.

These first nine, short chapters are the foundation on which we can better understand our brain on grief, navigate what's to come, take more efficient strides toward healing and eventually rebuild a life worth living.

After reading this section, feel free to read other sections and chapters as needed.

1

THE "RIGHT" WAY TO GRIEVE

After my loss, and as soon as my brain was able, I read a lot. Nothing made me angrier than reading about the stages of grief in a book written by someone who had never walked in my shoes. The stages of grief were never meant for those of us left behind (they were written for the dying), and the idea that there is a linear path forward, categorized by stages, just seemed so unrealistic to me. The hot mess of grief I was experiencing could never be organized neatly into stages—especially by someone who had not experienced such a life-shattering loss.

In addition to these unenlightening books and ideas, those of us who have lost a spouse often receive an onslaught of well-intended but extremely unhelpful comments like, "Time will heal," "You're young; you'll find someone else," and "You just need to accept this." Time doesn't heal, the single most frightening thought is that I have my whole life ahead of me, and no, I don't just need to accept this. *Please stop talking . . . you're adding to my misery.*

Later, in year two when the going gets (differently) tough, we hear, "You need to get over this," and "You really need to move on." *Seriously?*

Add to these external voices our own internal thoughts: *Shouldn't I be further along? What could I have done differently? Am I doing this right?* We compare ourselves to others and end up in despair.

From my perspective today, I would like to offer my take on the right way to grieve, and it is pretty simple: The right way to grieve is your way. On your timeline. No matter what anyone else says. The right way forward is the one that feels right to you.

There are about 350 million widowed people in the world[1] which means there are approximately 350 million right ways to grieve. The people who have opinions about the "right way" are very likely not among the 350 million.

But what if you're not sure whether your way is truly right for you?

You're more likely to find your own right way to grieve if you can let go of self-judgment. Forgive yourself for not knowing what you didn't know, for not doing what you didn't know to do. Let go of the guilt. Notice how often your thoughts include the word *should*. My guess is that if you're living with self-judgment, guilt, and lots of "shoulding," you're probably still searching for your right way.

You're more likely to find your own right way to grieve if you are ready to respond to those well-intended friends and family. One option is, "I appreciate your thoughts, but I am doing this my way."

You're more likely to find your own right way to grieve if you don't judge your response to life events. Ask yourself, "What am I making this mean?" For example, grief is the clumsy-one-step forward, two-steps-back shuffle of life after loss. The backward steps don't mean that you're doing it wrong.

Every day is different, and sometimes every minute is different. Some moments bring the most intense pain ever, and others offer happiness, even joy. If you're constantly on the wild roller-coaster ride of grief, it doesn't mean that you're doing it wrong.

It's okay if you can't remember simple things, if you can't read a short paragraph and understand it, and if you find your keys in the refrigerator. These are not signs that you're doing it wrong.

If you ugly cry in the hardware store and laugh out loud at a funny memory while at the cemetery, you're not doing it wrong.

If someone catches your eye or you have feelings for another person, especially if it is "way too soon" by societal standards, you're not doing it wrong.

On the other hand, if you are finding your way forward in a way that feels right for you, however slowly, then you're doing it right. If you are grieving on your terms and on your timeline, you're doing it right. If every day you just do your best, however imperfect, you're doing it right.

If all you can do is think of yourself as someone who is committed to finding your right way, you're already doing it right.

If you're committed to finding your right way to grieve the loss of your spouse, this book is for you. I hope this book will be your beacon of light and traveling companion as you find your way forward.

---

1. Sources Cited
   http://www.ipsnews.net/2020/02/widowhood-stressful-unprepared/

2

YOUR BRAIN ON GRIEF

In his award-winning book, *Live Long, Die Short: A Guide to Authentic Health and Successful Aging*, my friend Dr. Roger Landry says that we humans have version 1.0 brains and yet we live in a version 3.0 world.

Human brains are hard-wired in primitive ways, and their main objective is survival: preventing the possible tiger attack, eating in abundance because food might later be scarce, and never burning more calories than absolutely necessary.

Our primitive brain works to keep us alive in just three ways: by prompting us to (1) stay safe, (2) seek pleasure, and (3) be efficient. The humans whose brains did these tasks well survived and reproduced, and those of us living today are the recipients of primitive brains that are highly skilled at these three main tasks.

When our brain is chattering with messages of fear and scarcity, or laser-focusing on past events, or urging us to avoid pain by eating sugary treats, we can recognize that this is our primitive brain attempting to accomplish its main goal of keeping us alive through safety, pleasure, and efficiency.

If we were still living in a version 1.0 world with roaming tigers and scarce food sources, we could more easily appreciate the efforts of our primitive brains. However, we now live in a version 3.0 world (at least), and for people like us, struggling with the loss of our spouse, it is a world that has been shattered.

Luckily, over many generations our brains have developed the ability to do more than survive. Other parts of our brains have different functions. For example, the prefrontal cortex, unique to humans, is the part of the brain that can consider what's best in the long run, set goals, and help us achieve them. If the primitive brain is a toddler running around with a steak knife, then the prefrontal cortex is the adult in the room. When we learn to activate it, it will calm that toddler and put the knife in a safe place; in other words, the prefrontal cortex can counter the incessant chatter of the primitive brain.

When we are faced with tragedy, our world crumbles and the primitive brain takes the wheel. It operates in the protect-us-at-all-costs mode. We have experienced incredible trauma, and the primitive brain considers it equal to the tiger attack of days past. It studies the traumatic event from all angles in an attempt to prevent it from happening in the future. It sends fear messages to keep us safe at all times. It reminds us of our scarce situation: now lacking a spouse, possibly not having enough money, potentially not having the strength to go on. In the spirit of efficiency, our brain sends us the same messages again and again. After all, it would be inefficient to consider that something else might be true, and if there were ever a time to be efficient, it is during a crisis.

If this sounds familiar, know that nothing has gone wrong. This is your brain on grief. There are ways to navigate grief, but step one is to know that what you are experiencing is completely normal.

Chapter Summary

- Primitive human brains have one job, which is to keep us alive. They accomplish this in three ways: by prompting us to stay safe, seek pleasure, and be efficient.

- After our profound loss, our primitive brains take the wheel.
- Our prefrontal cortex is our "higher brain," which is designed to consider the long term, set goals, and help us achieve them. It can counterbalance the primitive brain.

Application

Grab a journal or your keyboard and write down some of the thoughts you are having today. Going forward, I'll refer to this activity as a *thought download*. Today as you write your thoughts, notice how they might be in line with one of the primitive brain's three main objectives.

In doing this regularly, you will learn to become a better eavesdropper on your brain. This skill will be key in your journey.

3

THE 50/50 MIX OF EMOTIONS

Kids are often told to "cheer up," "stop being afraid," or "don't be nervous." So it's no surprise that many people grow up thinking that difficult or negative emotions are not okay. What if instead we were taught that life is a 50/50 mix of positive and negative emotions?

What if we expected every single day to have its share of boredom, anxiety, and fear, and also happiness, peace, and laughter? What if we even expected our highly anticipated family vacation to be a 50/50 mix? It's going to be great, relaxing, and fun, and also, we will get on each other's nerves, worry that we will miss the flight, and disagree about what to eat for lunch.

If you've taken at least a few trips around the sun, you know that life isn't a bowl of cherries. There are some cherries, yes, but there are also the pits.

If we are not taught that approximately half of life is some form of difficult or negative emotion, then we are certainly not taught how to *have* these emotions: how to be with them until they pass, how to feel them fully, and how to process them completely.

Processing emotion is a superpower for two reasons. First, we can gain mastery over our emotions. We think that if we face a difficult emotion, it will consume us, but this is simply not true. When we are courageous enough to be fully present with a difficult emotion, it often loosens its grip. It shrinks to more normal proportions. Just like the most joyful emotions don't last forever, difficult emotions are temporary, too.

But processing emotion is a superpower for an even more important reason. Choosing to process a difficult emotion is to increase our willingness to feel any feeling. This is the ticket to the future you want to create for yourself.

Here is how to activate the superpower of processing emotion. Give yourself one to two minutes to feel the feeling.

1. Give it a name. What exactly are you feeling now? Sad? Lonely? Angry? Guilt or regret? If you can't quite name it, no problem. Skip to the next step.
2. Where is the feeling located in your body? Are you experiencing it in your chest, your shoulders, your stomach?
3. If it were a color, what color would the feeling be?
4. Would you describe it as hard or soft?
5. Is it fast or slow?
6. How does this feeling make you want to react?
7. Why are you having this feeling?
8. Take a few deep breaths. Breathe the feeling in. Repeat these steps again because the feeling will likely change in some way. Notice how the feeling changes.

Dedicating just one to two minutes to feeling a difficult emotion is a powerful experience. The best way through the pain is straight through. This is the superpower of processing emotion, which I hope you will do for yourself daily.

Chapter Summary

- Most people are not taught that life is a 50/50 mix of positive and negative emotion.
- Most people do not know how to be present with a negative emotion, which is also called processing an emotion.
- Processing an emotion is the simple act of staying with a feeling and describing it. To process an emotion is to activate a superpower.
- When we process an emotion, we are facing it fully, and it often results in (1) the emotion loosening its grip on us, however slightly; and (2) an increased willingness to feel any feeling.

Application

Take two minutes today to process an emotion. It can be a positive or negative emotion, but for now try to focus on a negative emotion. Trust that the feeling will not consume you but that, by you being fully present with it, the feeling will lessen, however slightly. Congratulate yourself for your willingness to feel a difficult feeling.

4

WHY CAN'T I STOP OVEREATING, OVERDRINKING, OVERSPENDING, OR BINGE-WATCHING?

In chapter 2 we learned that our primitive brain's main goal is to keep us alive. It does this in just three ways: by prompting us to (1) stay safe, (2) seek pleasure, and (3) be efficient.

In chapter 3 we learned that, generally speaking, life is a 50/50 mix of positive and negative emotions. Negative emotions come with the experience of being alive. It's perfectly normal to have a wide range of negative emotions, from bored to bummed out, from disappointed to distressed.

Yet our primitive brains equate negative, difficult, or uncomfortable emotions with potential danger. Negative emotions fly in the face of two of the three ways our brains attempt to keep us alive: by seeking pleasure and by seeking safety.

So rather than allow us to experience a negative emotion, primitive brains naturally urge us to find an escape button, whether by resisting it, reacting to it, or avoiding it.

Resisting emotions is to push them away, sweep them under the rug, or try to will ourselves to feel differently. We attempt to fake it until we make it.

Reacting to emotions is to snap, fly off the handle, or stay in bed all day because we think that the emotions are too tough to bear.

Avoiding an emotion is to attempt to buffer it with some sort of numbing agent. The brain convincingly suggests that, rather than feel the pain, we should escape it and seek pleasure instead. "Escapes" can include spending excessive time on social media, binging your favorite show, overeating, overdrinking, overspending, and viewing pornography, just to name a few. Yet these are false pleasures because each has its own negative consequence. I refer to engaging in this type of false pleasure as *buffering*.

The other problem with buffering is that negative feelings wait patiently. It simply isn't possible to successfully resist, react, or avoid to make our feelings go away. So when we turn to buffering, we now have to deal with the negative consequence of the false pleasure *and* the difficult emotion is still pursuing us, demanding our attention.

Now to this mix we add grief—an unprecedented level of difficult emotions. Soul-shattering. Unthinkable. Horrific. And, our primitive brains would have us think, unbearable.

So our primitive brains shift into overdrive, demanding that we hit the escape-button-of-choice like never before. We go on the run. We avoid. We react. We resist. We hold on to hope that, if we can stay on the run long enough, time will heal. And we wonder exactly how much time it will take.

My escape-button-of-choice was busy. At the time my husband passed away, I had a career that required significant travel. After days spent on the road, I came home to our ten acres that needed my attention and then I caught the next outbound plane. I was on the run for years, knowing that those emotions were just one step behind me, and fearing that they would overtake me.

I recently coached a wonderful person who was quite new to her grief. After her husband passed, she stayed busy with work. Later she retired and was busy with volunteer work and activities she enjoyed. It wasn't until the pandemic removed her escape button that her feelings caught up with her. Her husband had passed nearly thirty years ago. She ran in fear for thirty years, and yet those feelings were all still waiting for her, demanding her attention.

Time, by itself, does not heal.

There is no true escape from the difficult feelings that profound loss dumps on our lives.

There is no such thing as speed-grieving, but there is a more efficient way, which is to process difficult emotions as we learned in the previous chapter.

Reaching for an external solution to an internal problem simply does not work.

So, if you've felt like a failure with every pound gained, dollar spent, and episode binged, please recognize that you are actually not failing. In reality, your primitive brain is in overdrive, doing its job, keeping you seeking pleasure, keeping you "safe," and doing it all on repeat, which is its way of being efficient.

Next time your brain insists that you urgently reach for your escape-button-of-choice, simply follow the suggestions in this chapter's application section.

Facing your feelings is one of the most courageous things you can do in life, and especially in life after loss.

Chapter Summary

- Our primitive brains are hardwired with the sole goal of keeping us alive, and they achieve this by prompting us to (1) stay safe, (2) seek pleasure, and (3) be efficient.
- When life serves up difficult emotions, our primitive brains equate these emotions to potential danger and therefore urge us to escape our feelings.
- Our escape-button-of-choice typically has its own negative

consequence, and it can't even permanently erase the feeling we are trying to avoid. This is why it's called a *false pleasure*.
- Time alone does not heal. The most efficient way through grief is to process the feelings.

Application

When you have an urge to escape difficult feelings by reaching for your preferred false pleasure, ask yourself, *What feeling am I not wanting to feel right now?* Allow that urge to be there, without reaching for the false pleasure, for just two minutes. During those two minutes, revisit chapter 3 and walk through the steps to process an emotion. After two minutes, decide whether you still want to reach for the false pleasure. Don't expect perfection. It's a journey.

5

FACTS ARE DIFFERENT THAN THOUGHTS

"Never believe everything you think." —Unknown

In chapter 2 I discussed becoming a better eavesdropper on your thoughts. In this chapter, I want to teach you how to question them.

Most people are not taught to question their thoughts. Thoughts are simply sentences that our brains are offering us, and they just seem true. In reality, thoughts are easily mistaken for facts, and therein lies great opportunity for growth.

Separating facts from thoughts is a powerful and potentially life-changing exercise. The first step is to really understand the meaning of *fact*. A fact is a statement that can be proven in a court of law, and all people on earth would agree on it.

A spouse died. Sister-in-law sent a text message. I live in the house we shared. These are facts.

He should never have died in that way. She was so disrespectful. I'm all alone. These are thoughts.

Another example is body weight. The number on the scale is a fact. It can be recorded and proven in a court of law, and everyone on earth would agree that the scale does in fact say the specific number. How we interpret the number is a thought. We tend to make the number mean that we're overweight and unhealthy and less worthy than someone who weighs twenty pounds less than we do.

Separating facts from thoughts is powerful because although the facts are the facts—unchangeable and outside of our control—our thoughts *about* the facts are always 100% optional and within our control. As we learn to be keen observers of our thoughts, we can begin to question what else might be true. We can begin to observe how each thought plays out in our lives (more on that to come). We can become fierce editors of our thoughts. This is the path forward.

Chapter Summary

- We often mistakenly believe our thoughts are factual, but there is a difference between thoughts and facts.
- A fact can be proven in a court of law, and everyone on earth would agree it is true. If the sentence in your brain doesn't meet that definition, it is a thought.
- Thoughts are not always true or useful, but they are always 100% optional.

Application

Download your thoughts and circle the ones that are facts based on the definition in this chapter. The rest are thoughts. Can you see how your thoughts may not be true? Consider that other thoughts might also be true. Are you willing to be wrong about your current thoughts?

6

THOUGHTS CREATE FEELINGS

Thoughts are sentences that our brains offer us. As we learned in the previous chapter, they are not the same as facts, they are not always true, and sometimes our thoughts don't serve us.

Next, let's consider feelings. We think that our circumstances (the facts of our lives) cause our feelings: She made me feel guilty. That presentation made me so anxious. I have so much guilt because of his death.

But the truth is that our circumstances never *directly* cause our feelings. Our thoughts *about* the circumstances create our feelings, and this is very good news because thoughts are always optional.

Let's revisit those statements and notice how it is actually our thoughts about the facts that create our feelings.

She said words (fact) that made me think thoughts that caused me to feel guilty.

The presentation on my schedule (fact) caused me to think that I wasn't prepared enough (thought), so I felt anxious (feeling).

He passed away (fact), and I believe that I should have been there (thought), so I feel guilty (feeling).

That thoughts create feelings is good news because once we know this, we are no longer victims of our circumstances. No one has the power to make us feel terrible. The past has no power over us because the circumstances are now in the past; only our thoughts about them today can cause us pain in the present.

Now, I'm not suggesting that we should feel nothing but good feelings at all times. Life in general is not a walk in the park, much less life after loss. Life, in fact, is a 50/50 mix of positive and negative emotions—and that's perfectly okay.

Sometimes our most authentic thoughts do create difficult, negative emotions. We want to feel sad when someone we love dies. Negative feelings are not a problem; they are what make us human.

The most authentic human experience is to feel the wide variety of emotions: positive and negative, joyful and sad, thrilled and bored, brave and afraid, wonderful and weak.

This array of feelings is created not by circumstances but by your thoughts about the circumstances. Therein lies your power.

Chapter Summary

- The circumstances (facts) that happen in our lives have no power to make us feel anything.
- It is our thoughts about our circumstances that cause our feelings.
- Life is a 50/50 mix of positive and negative emotions. Negative emotions are not a problem.

Application

Download your thoughts and notice how each makes you feel. Or conversely, notice how you are feeling and ask yourself what thoughts you are thinking. Be sure to tease out the facts from the thoughts.

1. Circumstance (fact)

2. Thought
3. Feeling

7

FEELINGS PROMPT ACTION OR INACTION

Every action you have ever taken was fueled by a feeling. Every action (or inaction) you will take today will be prompted by how you are feeling in that moment. Every action you will ever take in the future will be driven by how you feel at the time.

Feelings produce action, and this is great news because we already know that our thoughts create our feelings and that our thoughts are always within our control. So, if we can think authentic thoughts that generate any feeling, and if feelings prompt action, we have even more control over our lives than we ever thought.

Let's look to the past to see how this concept is true. Perhaps you have a college degree. You were able to get that degree only because at one point, you believed that you could (thought). That thought created a feeling—maybe you felt motivated. From the feeling of motivation, you took many actions: attended classes, studied for exams, saw a tutor, wrote the paper, completed an internship, and so on. In reality, each of those specific actions was probably generated by a slightly different feeling. But in the end, those actions accumulated and resulted in your degree. You accomplished this goal because you once had a thought that you could do it, resulting in feelings that drove actions.

Now let's focus on today. What if you exercised because you actually wanted to? What if you felt excited to take that painting class? What if you were truly motivated to eat healthier meals? All of this—and so much more—is possible when we harness the complete control we have over our lives. It starts with a thought.

When thinking about the future, you may feel unable to take action. Why? Because you are feeling insecure, uncertain, unsafe, or perhaps incapable. Those are feelings that (like all feelings) are happening due to your thoughts. These thoughts may or may not be true, but we can say for sure that they are not serving you because they generate a feeling that keeps you stuck. When thinking about the future (which is covered in depth later in this book) it's essential to find a thought that is completely true for you, which will generate a feeling that prompts the action that you want to take. This process works every time.

Chapter Summary

- Feelings (which are caused by thoughts) prompt action or inaction.
- Any action (or inaction) of the past or present is the result of our feelings at the time.
- Since thoughts are in our control, we can choose thoughts that are true to us and that create feelings that will naturally prompt actions we want to take.

Application

Reflect on an action you have taken in the past. What feeling caused that action? Think about actions you are taking now. What feelings are prompting these actions? When you consider actions you want to take in the future, what will you need to feel in order to do so?

8

ACTIONS BECOME RESULTS

The actions we take, big and small, add up to results. Similarly, the actions we don't take add up to results.

For example, you notice a painting class being offered in your area. You think you'd like to try it, and you feel excited. You look online at the date and time and make a list of the materials you need to buy. You pay the fee, mark your calendar, pick up the necessary supplies, and eventually get in the car and drive to your first class. You listen to the instruction, mix colors, and put paintbrush to canvas. Ultimately you end up with a painting—the result of your many actions.

Inactions also add up to results. Although most of us acknowledge that we should eat healthfully and exercise, we often choose inaction instead. Not buying the healthy foods, not meal prepping, not going for a walk or hitting the gym after work. These actions we don't take add up to results that we don't want—typically added pounds or chronic health conditions.

As we learned in the previous chapter, all actions (or inactions) are fueled by our feelings. And all feelings are created by our thoughts. So, when we are not taking a desired action, we can ask ourselves what thoughts and feelings are prompting our current, undesirable actions. In addition, notice the result the action or inaction has created.

To change our actions, we need to decide what feeling would prompt the desired action. Then we must consider what thought would create that feeling. Finally, we can direct our brains to choose that thought.

Chapter Summary

- Thoughts create feelings, and feelings prompt action or inaction.
- The actions we take (or don't take) add up to results, for better or worse.
- When taking undesirable actions, ask yourself what thoughts and feelings are prompting those actions. Notice the result the actions are creating.
- Choosing desirable actions requires finding the thought that will create the feeling that will prompt the desirable actions.

Application

Think about some of your past results—for example achieving a college degree, marrying your spouse, getting a promotion at work, or gaining excess weight, starting to smoke again, or becoming a hoarder. What actions created the result? What feelings prompted you to take those actions? What thoughts created those feelings?

You can do this same exercise for the results you have presently and to start creating the results you want in the future.

9

PAIN VERSUS SUFFERING

While the words *pain* and *suffering* are often used interchangeably, for the purpose of this book, I'd like to make an important distinction.

Pain is the uncomfortable emotion that comes with being alive. It's what we experience when we lose our spouse, among other difficult life events. We feel pain when we miss our spouse's physical presence and mourn our shared past and planned future.

Suffering, on the other hand, is the uncomfortable emotion that we manufacture in our minds and pile on top of the pain. Suffering is unnecessary and extremely common.

Every feeling we humans experience comes from our thoughts. Any time you feel an uncomfortable emotion, notice what thoughts you are currently thinking. Write the thoughts down and ask yourself, "Is this true?" and "Is this useful?"

It is shocking to discover how often our brains offer us thoughts that are neither true nor useful. Even if a thought is true, if it isn't useful, then it isn't serving you.

Thoughts create feelings, and feelings prompt actions (or inactions) that create our results. So, our thoughts ultimately show up as results, for better or worse.

The two questions “Is this thought true?” and “Is this thought useful?” will help you distinguish between pain and suffering. If you answer no to either of those questions, the thought you are thinking is very likely creating suffering.

Here is a nuance: thoughts that produce pain that comes with the loss of a spouse are actually useful thoughts. They create what is sometimes called “clean pain.” Processing pain, as we learned in chapter 3, is the most efficient way through. For example, thoughts like “I miss his hugs,” and “I miss us,” will likely create feelings of sadness. This is an emotion that we can be present with in order to process it.

Alternatively, thoughts like, “I should be further along by now,” “I should have been able to save him,” and “I’m not grieving correctly,” as well as other forms of self-judgment all create suffering. These thoughts are often neither true (meaning factual per the definition in chapter 5) nor useful. They create feelings that cannot be processed and instead keep us stuck, spinning in the darkness, looping in suffering.

Every human’s superpower is the ability to choose thoughts. Thoughts are 100% optional. If your thoughts are not *both* true *and* useful, ask yourself, “What else might be true?” It is entirely possible to direct our brains to select thoughts that ultimately create the results we seek. Choosing our thoughts is how we can deal with suffering.

The distinction between pain and suffering is an important waypoint in navigating life after loss.

Chapter Summary

- Pain that comes with great loss is pain that we need to process.
- Suffering comes from untrue/unhelpful thoughts that our brains offer us.
- We can learn to become fierce editors of those thoughts—

deleting them and choosing alternate thoughts that are 100% true and useful.

Application

Do a thought download to see what your brain is offering you today.

Sometimes it's easier to download our thoughts when we are experiencing an emotion. We can ask ourselves, "Why am I feeling this way?" The answer will be thoughts that we can then write down and examine.

Notice whether your thoughts fall into the category of pain or suffering.

THE PAST

An important waypoint in the journey of life after loss is reconciling the events of the past. The burden of a painful past can add significantly to the weight of grief and keep us firmly stuck in the darkness. I help my coaching clients reframe a difficult past, including the regrets that go hand in hand with loss.

By reconciling a painful past, we have more bandwidth to navigate the present and eventually create a future that is certainly not what we had planned, yet still incredibly meaningful and beautiful.

10

POWER OVER THE PAST

The past can be truly horrific. There were mistakes, difficult situations, dark secrets, failures and challenges, and then there was the death of a spouse. As much as we might desperately wish we could change the past, it is never possible. We can expend tremendous energy rethinking and overanalyzing, trying to find a way to renegotiate past events, grappling with what is, wrestling with reality. It's exhausting, and energy spent this way quickly depletes the finite, microscopic energy levels that most people have after loss.

I like the notion that we feel no old pain from the past. It's our current thinking *about* the past that inflicts pain. Our thoughts create our feelings, so it's important to learn to observe our own thoughts. What are our brains telling us about the past, are these thoughts true, and do they serve the person we are today? If not, perhaps there is a new thought about the past that would still be true, and also more useful.

For example, let's consider that a spouse died by suicide (which is a fact). "He shouldn't have ended his life," might be a thought that causes extreme pain for many years. What else might be true? Perhaps, "He was in tremendous pain and must have believed there was no other option." Any replacement thoughts must feel 100% true to you. Finding different thoughts is not about unicorns-and-rainbows-type thinking but about taking control of your brain and choosing thoughts that are still true for you, yet less hurtful.

Widowed or not, we can easily define ourselves and our future abilities based on our past. But that would be a big mistake. What if at age sixteen you were limited to only your past abilities? That wouldn't make sense because you would have so much growth still ahead of you. It is tragic that we decide at some random point in our lives that we can no longer grow.

If we choose to see everything in our past as simply lessons and preparation, this viewpoint can be a launchpad to becoming the next version of ourselves. A painful event like the loss of a spouse is not what we had planned or hoped for, certainly. But it is what happened. Our hearts are still beating, and we are living this one life we have been given.

We've already been through the unimaginable, and it has, in its own dark and messy way, prepared us for what's next. Let's not be limited by the past, or carry around unnecessary pain from the past. Might now be the time to become who we are meant to be—not in spite of the past—but because of it?

Chapter Summary

- Reconciling the past is a key waypoint in the journey of life after loss.
- There is no "old pain" from the past. There are only thoughts we have about the past, which create pain.
- Our abilities are not defined by the past.
- Past events have been lessons and preparation—a launchpad for the future version of you.

Application

Write a letter to your past self. In it, finish these sentences:

I'm angry because . . .

I'm sad because . . .

I wish . . .

I'm sorry that . . .

I love you because . . .

Another great exercise is to download your thoughts about your past. Notice which statements are factual; the rest are thoughts. Notice which thoughts create suffering. Ask yourself what else might be true, and then try those thoughts "on for size" and see how each one makes you feel. When you find true thoughts that don't create suffering, you'll want to practice those thoughts daily. See the Belief Plan exercise at the end of this section.

11

GOT GUILT?

Guilt and grief seem to go hand in hand, yet I have rarely found a book, article, or other resource that addresses the guilt many of us experience. Guilt seems to come in three varieties, guilt about the past, guilt in the present, and guilt when we think about the future.

Guilt (or any feeling) comes from the thoughts we think or from our beliefs (which are thoughts we have consistently thought). You've probably heard the saying, "Don't believe everything you think." The truth is that we have many thoughts and beliefs that are simply not true and that are definitely not serving us.

Thoughts that produce the feeling of guilt include, "I should have known he was suicidal," "I should have been able to save him," "I complained about the coffee he brought me in the morning," and "I was short-tempered with him," just to name a few. When you feel guilty about the past, it's a great practice to write down the thoughts you're thinking.

Maya Angelou is quoted as saying, "Forgive yourself for not knowing what you didn't know before you learned it."[1] Isn't that what you would tell a good friend who is feeling guilty about the past? If only we can learn to show ourselves the same kindness and understanding that we show to our friends.

Present-tense guilt may come from thoughts such as, "I should not feel happy because that's an insult to my spouse," or "I did something for myself that he would not have approved of." Thinking about the future or the next steps in our healing also brings about guilt. "I'd love to have companionship," or "I'd like to date again," or "I'm ready to live for me," are all thoughts that can dish out large servings of guilt. Why? Because those thoughts are contrary to our current beliefs about loss. Perhaps we believe that dating again would be cheating, that fully living again would be an insult, or that the length of our misery should somehow represent our love for our spouse.

Beliefs are simply the thoughts we often think, and they can be hard to notice because they usually fly under the radar. When you feel guilt, examine the thoughts you are thinking. What beliefs do you hold in your mind? Then, question whether your beliefs are actually true and whether they are your own, are current, and are serving this version of you.

The good news is that we always get to choose our thoughts about the past, present, and future, and from there we can build new beliefs that not only serve us today but also serve the person we are becoming.

Because we can choose our thoughts, guilt is optional. Guilt is suffering that our brains manufacture, and then this suffering is piled on top of the pain of our loss. As if the pain weren't already enough.

Guilt is heavy. And it's optional.

Chapter Summary

- Guilt can go hand in hand with grief.
- Guilt is a feeling, and like all feelings, it is produced by our thoughts.
- Beliefs are thoughts we have thought often. We feel guilty when we are not aligned with our beliefs. Yet most thoughts/beliefs go unquestioned.

- Thoughts/beliefs are sometimes neither true nor useful.
- Guilt about the past, present, and future are common with grief.

Application

Download every thought that produces guilt for you. For each thought, ask yourself what else is true. What if the opposite were actually true? Bookmark this chapter for use later in this section when we create a Belief Plan.

---

1. https://www.mayaangelou.com/

12

WRESTLING WITH REALITY

This should have never happened. He should be here. We should be living out the future we planned.

Sound familiar?

Whether we were widowed unexpectedly or knew it was coming, many of us struggle to accept our horrible new reality.

So we argue with what is. We rail against our circumstances. We wrestle with our horrific new existence. It's an exhausting battle that we can never win because, no matter how much we fight, reality is still reality. Although this struggle is a normal part of grief, when we stay in this place long-term, we stay stuck. We pile suffering on top of our pain.

We resist accepting what is, in part, because of what we make acceptance mean. Our brains tell us that accepting what is means that we are letting go of our spouse, or that we are condoning what has happened.

But in truth, acceptance only means that we agree that the loss did, in fact, happen. His heart stopped beating. We don't like it; we would give anything to change it, but it most certainly did happen.

By agreeing with the fact that it did happen, we are deciding to redirect our energy. We choose to focus that microscopic amount of energy with which we find ourselves each day on other areas that matter to us, that need our attention.

In redirecting our energy, we end this particular variety of suffering. And maybe then we can take a little better care of ourselves, we can better process our pain, or we can begin to understand how to put one foot in front of the other.

Acceptance isn't just one, irreversible decision. Today you can decide to practice acceptance and tomorrow you might want to go back to wrestling with reality. Sometimes we just want to argue with it. There is no right or wrong. Just notice how you feel when you're arguing with reality, observe your energy levels, and know that you have a choice to think other thoughts on purpose.

Chapter Summary

- Struggling to accept your new reality is common and perfectly okay.
- Arguing with reality feels terrible and utilizes a great deal of our limited energy.
- Accepting reality doesn't mean we like it; it only means that the loss did, in fact, happen.
- Acceptance is a choice we make by directing our thoughts.

Application

Download all your thoughts about your loss. Write about why it shouldn't have happened, how it shouldn't have happened the way it did, and so on. Many clients tell me that they "did it wrong" in the final moments of their spouse's life. If that thought feels true for you, in what ways did you do it "wrong?" Get it all out. Wrestle with reality as much as you would like. Sometimes just getting these thoughts out onto paper is helpful.

Examples: *He was too young. He deserved to enjoy his retirement. He had so much life yet to live. I should have seen the signs. I should have been able to save him.*

Notice how these thoughts make you feel.

Next, challenge yourself to consider other thoughts that are also true for you.

Examples: *He died exactly the way he wanted to—without warning. He didn't suffer / he is no longer suffering. He lived fully every day of his life. I could not have done anything different. I did my best given what I knew at the time.*

Notice how these thoughts make you feel. You may want to integrate some of your notes from this chapter into the Belief Plan exercise at the end of this section.

13

WHY YOU DON'T HAVE TO LET HIM GO

Perhaps you've been told by a well-intentioned person that it's time to "let him go." As if that is a necessary step in the journey or some unwritten requirement for grieving "correctly."

Or maybe this is something you tell yourself. That, in order to move forward, you've got to leave him in the past.

In my work as a life coach, I've had conversations with hundreds of widowed people, and this notion comes up regularly. "It's time to let him go" is a thought. For many people, it's a thought that causes suffering because it makes us feel terrible, guilt-ridden, and just plain sad.

Anytime a thought causes extra suffering, we can examine it in greater detail. Is the thought true? Is it useful? What if the opposite were true?

Thoughts are always 100% optional. Our brains offer us tens of thousands of thoughts a day. Some are true, and some are not. Some serve us well, while others cause us to suffer. Our job is to become fierce editors of our thoughts: keeping the ones that are true and useful, and upgrading the rest.

I would offer that "letting him go" is a thought with a lot of potential to cause unnecessary hurt.

Personally, I have never let my late husband go. I have accepted the reality of his passing, and I have done each day since his passing with him and for him (and for me). He is as much a part of me now as he was then. He is as much a part of my days, my thoughts, my struggles, and my wins. I could see no way to deconstruct us, so letting him go never seemed possible.

Even as I have taken significant strides forward, allowed my heart to gain new capacity to love, and committed to creating a future with a new love, my late husband has been a part of all of it. Because he is forever a part of me.

Chapter Summary

- The notion of "letting him go" is advice we receive from others and can be something we tell ourselves that we must do. It's just not true.
- "Letting him go" is a thought that creates unnecessary suffering.
- Thoughts are optional. The opposite thought might also be true for you: that you never have to "let him go."

Application

Take a moment to consider the following questions and then write the answers down in your journal. Keep what you have written so you can refer to it in the future if your brain continues to offer the thought that you must "let him go."

In what ways do you believe your spouse is still with you?

How might you move forward with your spouse?

In what ways can you live your life for your spouse, and for you?

How might your life be a tribute to your spouse?

In what ways might you live enough for the both of you?

14

WHY YOU DON'T HAVE TO "MOVE ON"

In the last chapter I busted the popular grief myth that you must "let him go" in order to properly grieve. Now we'll tackle an equally popular and well-intentioned bit of advice: "It's time to move on."

This statement implies that we should leave the past in the past, accept reality, and stop wallowing, because by societal standards, after all, it's time. You've had "enough" time to grieve. Now you need to move on, if for no other reason, so that the people who care about you can stop worrying. If you're "moving on," everyone else won't have to experience the awkwardness of trying to support you. It'll just be better for everyone. Please, just move on.

The problem is that "moving on" is akin to "letting him go." It feels horrible. Many widowed people interpret moving on as disregarding their person, their marriage, their shared past and planned future. They feel that moving on would be like hitting delete on all the things that have meant everything. It's leaving him in the past.

Personally, I have never moved on.

I have put one foot in front of the other. I have moved forward with him and for him. I have allowed myself to dream again. I have considered how I might live a life big enough for the two of us. I have taken significant steps toward that life.

I'm proof that "moving on" is not a requirement. It's simply a thought. While it might be a thought that serves some people, for many it simply doesn't work. It causes extra, unnecessary suffering. It makes us feel awful.

Yet thoughts, as you know, are always 100% optional. When one doesn't work for us, we can ask ourselves what else is true. What if the opposite were true? Try on different thoughts that feel true to you, and find ones that make you feel peaceful, confident, and purposeful (or any other feeling that you want to feel).

Because if life can be brutal, then it can also be beautiful. Even life after loss. Especially life after loss.

Chapter Summary

- "Moving on" is not a requirement in life after loss.
- "Moving on" is simply a thought, and it's one that makes many people feel awful.
- Moving forward is possible and doesn't require that we leave our spouse in the past.

Application

Notice how the thought of "moving on" feels for you. Notice how the thought of "moving forward" feels. Brainstorm ways that you might move forward with your spouse. How might you live your life in his honor? For some, it is tackling a bucket list of adventures that he wanted to experience. For others, it's living a big life just for you as you evolve into this new version of yourself. Try on options and see what seems right for you.

15

FINDING FREEDOM IN FORGIVENESS

Forgiveness can be tough, right? I used to think so. We liken it to condoning behavior or accepting an apology—tough pills to swallow. But it is neither of those things.

Forgiveness is simply deciding to stop feeling angry and resentful. That's it.

The only action that forgiveness requires is our own personal decision to stop feeling angry and resentful (and then to take a few surprisingly simple steps, which I will share.)

No other actions are necessary, including the following:

- Having a conversation with the other person
- Telling them that you've forgiven them
- Accepting an apology from someone
- Allowing someone back into your life
- Condoning behavior

Those actions are all optional when it comes to forgiveness—optional, not mandatory.

Forgiveness is truly an inside job. The only person who needs to know that you've forgiven someone is you. Forgiveness is just another name for freedom: freedom from anger and resentment.

American author Jonathan Lockwood Huie is quoted as saying, "Forgive others, not because they deserve forgiveness, but because you deserve peace."[1]

When is the right time to forgive? Only you can decide when you are ready to let go of anger and resentment. Sometimes we just want to feel those feelings, and that's okay. Just know that the other person does not experience your anger and resentment—only you do. Also know that your anger and resentment do not punish the other person. They punish only you.

As the old saying goes, withholding forgiveness is like drinking poison and waiting for the other person to get sick.

A powerful question to ask yourself is whether you like how anger and resentment feel or if you are ready to shed those feelings. You always have the choice, and if you want to, you can make that choice today.

First, let's understand why we feel anger and resentment.

The person's words or actions happened. Then we have a thought about them. That thought creates how we feel. We feel anger and resentment because of what we are thinking about the person and their actions. To us, our thoughts seem absolutely true, but they are not serving us because they create anger and resentment.

While the person's words or actions are outside of your control, your thoughts about them are completely within your control. This means that the person actually has no power over you. Your power is in your thinking.

How to Forgive

1. Consider the person's words or actions and write down all the thoughts you have about them. Notice that these thoughts create anger and resentment.

2. Next, ask your brain to consider what *other* thoughts might also be true. Now, your brain won't want to do this work because it is committed to the current thoughts and is certain that they are true. Simply ask your brain to imagine possibilities. There are no right or wrong answers. Just make a list. Here are some possibilities to consider:

- Hurt people sometimes hurt people.
- She/he did the best they could given what they knew at the time.
- Just because she/he doesn't love me the way I would like, doesn't mean that they don't love me with all they have.
- It was always supposed to happen this way.
- It was painful, and yet it shaped me into who I am today.

3. Review your list of new thoughts. Try each thought on like you would an outfit. Discover how each makes you feel. Select the ones that feel true and that create a feeling that you want to feel. Choose thoughts that feel better than anger and resentment.

Brains are creatures of habit. Your brain will likely still offer you the well-practiced thoughts of the past, and you will then feel anger and resentment creep back into your life. That's to be expected. This exercise is your chance to redirect your brain toward the new thoughts that you created and tested in step 3.

Over time, these new thoughts will become your default thinking.

Welcome to the freedom of forgiveness.

Remember to forgive yourself, too.

Chapter Summary

- Forgiveness is simply deciding to stop feeling angry and resentful.

- Forgiveness is solely an inside job—one that doesn't require any external action.
- Anger and resentment come from our thoughts about the other person's actions.
- Forgiveness is a three-step process.
- New thoughts will require practice.

Application

If you are ready to stop carrying anger and resentment, write the name of the person you would like to forgive. What were their actions or words? What are your thoughts *about* their actions/words? How do these thoughts make you feel?

If you don't want to continue to feel this way, ask your brain to come up with other thoughts that are still true for you but that produce different feelings.

In what ways have you not yet forgiven yourself?

---

1. https://www.jonathanlockwoodhuie.com/quotes/inspirational/

16

BELIEFS, ON PURPOSE

One reason we stay stuck spiraling in the past is that our brains are made for efficiency. The main goal of our primitive human brain is to keep us alive, and one way the brain accomplishes this goal is by being efficient. When it comes to our thoughts, efficiency equals redundancy.

Our brains offer us the same thoughts, day in and day out. We tend to believe that everything we think is true, so most thoughts go unexamined.

Thoughts we think over and over again become beliefs. In the spirit of efficiency, our brains file our beliefs in the subconscious. It is inefficient, after all, to consciously rethink things that we already believe to be true.

In the chapters we have covered so far, we have learned

- that all thoughts are 100% optional.
- that thoughts are simply sentences in our minds.
- that our thoughts are sometimes not true.
- that our thoughts sometimes don't serve us.

In previous chapters, I recommend becoming a better observer of your own thoughts, then learning to question each one. The goal is to realize that you are not your thoughts and to eventually become a fierce editor of what your brain is offering you. Because unmonitored, unquestioned thoughts running on repeat can become a self-imposed prison sentence.

In a life that has suddenly and irreversibly spun out of control, thought management becomes our first opportunity to *regain* control. Although our brains might be offering one thought on repeat, a host of other thoughts are also true.

We can direct our brains to think thoughts that are both true and useful. Choosing new thoughts is how we unlock the handcuffs and step into new possibility.

Since our thoughts directly create our feelings, and since our thoughts are 100% optional, it is best to choose thoughts that don't make us feel horrible. After all, this life is tough enough (understatement of the year) without our brains manufacturing unnecessary additional suffering.

I encourage my coaching clients to create a Belief Plan, and I hope you will create one for yourself. (In fact, I recommend that you create a belief plan for your past, present, and future.)

A Belief Plan is a list of thoughts that are true for you and that serve you. The list can also include thoughts that you want to believe but don't quite believe yet. It does not include thoughts that you do not believe at all. No unicorns, no rainbows, just truth.

Here is an example of a Belief Plan about the past. (Note: Not all these thoughts will ring true for you or serve you, but feel free to use the ones that do.) I've included common thoughts that create suffering, along with a corresponding thought that a person might find equally true and—here's what's important—creates a more useful feeling. Finally, I've added a column for a 1–10 rating, where 10 indicates very strong belief.

This Belief Plan is just an example. I encourage you to create your own using this format. Glance back over your notes from the past few chapters' Application sections. List your common thoughts that feel terrible and then make a specific note of how each thought makes you feel. Next, ask your brain what else is true and useful and then note what feeling that new thought creates. Finally, rate how strongly you believe the new thoughts.

Common thought	Feeling it creates	New thought (must be true)	Feeling it creates	Belief rating (1–10)
I should have been able to save him.	*regret*	*I did the best I could given what I knew at the time.*	*peace*	8
He should have never done that.	*resentment*	*Hurt people tend to hurt people.*	*compassionate*	7
She should have known better.	*anger*	*We humans are messy.*	*accepting*	10
I could have been a better wife.	*ashamed*	*Wives, husbands, and marriages are never perfect.*	*imperfectly normal*	9
He should have loved me more.	*rejected*	*Just because he didn't love me the way I wanted to be loved, doesn't mean that he didn't love me with all he had.*	*loved*	9
This should have never happened to a child.	*victimized*	*The difficulties of childhood prepared me with skills for adulthood.*	*resilient*	7

Chapter Summary

- Beliefs are thoughts that we think over and over again.
- The brain files beliefs away in the subconscious, making them a bit harder to identify.
- A Belief Plan is a list of thoughts that are both true and useful.

Application

Create your own Belief Plan focusing on the past. (You will create a separate one for the present and the future in subsequent chapters.) But creating the plan is not enough. You'll also need to regularly recite the new thoughts you have created.

Just as the Pledge of Allegiance and the Lord's Prayer are recitations of beliefs, the list of new thoughts you made in your Belief Plan can become a recitation practice. I recommend that you recite it at least daily, or more often as needed. Pause after you say each thought so you can feel the feeling that the thought creates. Notice whether your belief rating gradually increases. Over time, modify your Belief Plan as needed.

Now, just because you've created a Belief Plan and have recited your new thoughts a few times does not mean that your brain won't still offer you old thoughts. Over the years, your brain has built superhighways to your old, well-practiced thoughts. When we create new thoughts that serve us better, we are blazing a new trail. The more we think the new thoughts on purpose, the sooner we'll have a dirt road, then a one-lane paved road, and so on. Eventually we will develop superhighways to the new thoughts that serve us (and the old, rarely traveled superhighway will waste away).

It's not a problem that your brain offers you old thoughts. Acknowledge them as normal, and then direct your brain to think your new Belief Plan thoughts on purpose.

THE PRESENT

What is most difficult for you right now? The chapters in this book are labeled so that you can skip to the specific information you need today. The first few chapters will help you be "on to" your brain's natural tendencies during this difficult time. Understanding the normalcy of fear, scarcity, overwhelm, and a focus on negativity can help us understand ourselves better—which can be a big relief.

An important skill in navigating life after loss is observation without judgment. Notice what is happening in your life but refrain from deciding if it is good or bad, appropriate or not. It just is. Practice saying to yourself, "Okay, this is what we've got today." Crying by 8 a.m.? Okay, this is what we've got today. Two steps forward, five steps back? Okay, this is what we've got today.

Another strategy is thinking about your day using the preface "Oh, this is the part when. . . . " An example is, "Oh, this is the part when I sob at the grocery store." It just is. Judging yourself isn't useful. Accepting your grief process as it is will help you redirect your limited bandwidth to the specific areas of your life that need healing. Remember to observe without judging.

17

THE FEAR FACTOR

C. S. Lewis wrote, "No one ever told me that grief felt so like fear," and he went on to describe the way he physically experienced the sensation of grief, which for him, was similar to the sensation of fear.[1]

After I lost my husband, grief and fear were one. They were welded together so seamlessly that I couldn't tell them apart. I lived in fear. I made decisions out of fear. I looked at most people as a threat. I feared everything about the future. Fear ruled my life after loss so completely, yet I never recognized the feeling as fear. I just called it grief.

Our human brains are hardwired with three main objectives: to keep us safe, to keep us comfortable, and to be efficient. Profound loss turns these most basic objectives into near impossible tasks. With the loss of our spouse, our primitive brain is shaken as if we were just attacked by a tiger. The brain perceives the loss as a threat and launches into danger-zone mode.

Our brain analyzes the events associated with our loss, replays them, and studies them from every angle in an effort to relate the event to something understandable, something in the past, or something that makes sense. It loops on these difficult events to try to protect us from ever experiencing such “danger” again. It’s no wonder “widow brain” is so common.

In an effort to keep us comfortable, our primitive brains avoid the dark, difficult, and unfamiliar feelings that come with loss. We find other things to do instead, like overeating, overdrinking, overspending, Netflix binging, and the like. But grief is patient; it waits for us. And while it waits, it grows. We can run, but we can’t hide.

Our primitive brain plays a significant role in the decisions we make in our life after loss. As it seeks to keep us safe and comfortable, it tells us to stay away from anything that is not familiar because it perceives anything new as potentially unsafe. In an effort to do its job, our primitive brain keeps us stuck in the quicksand of grief.

Luckily, only part of our brain is primitive in nature. Another part of our brain called the prefrontal cortex is wired differently, and it helps us to override primitive messages. But there’s a catch: we have to approach our primitive brain carefully, without judgment, and with compassion and kindness. It goes something like this:

“I hear you, primitive brain. I can see that you’re doing your job. Your opinion is noted. But we’re going to do this instead. We’re going to try this new thing. We’re going to entertain new thoughts. And although you are sensing danger, we are actually okay.”

With this dialogue, we can take small steps into life after loss. We can stop looping in pain, guilt, and fear. We can slowly reconstruct our identity and create a live that we love.

Chapter Summary

- Grief and fear often go hand in hand
- The primitive part of the human brain has only one job: to keep us safe.
- The primitive brain is shaken by loss; therefore, it launches into overdrive, sensing danger everywhere.

- Another part of the brain, the prefrontal cortex, can override these messages of fear.

Application

What scares you? What do you fear? Do a thought download of all the sentences in your brain that cause fear. Are they thoughts about people? Situations? The future? Not all of them will be logical, and that's okay. Just write it all down without filtering or editing.

Notice that these thoughts are coming from your primitive brain in an effort to keep you alive. Practice acknowledging your primitive brain and then using your prefrontal cortex to decide which fears are rational. This is a skill that you can develop over time.

Also, be on the lookout for fear-based thoughts this week. Notice how often your brain offers you such thoughts. Observe without judgment. It's just your primitive brain trying to do its job.

---

1. Lewis, C. S. (1968). A grief observed. London: Faber & Faber.

18

IS FAMILIAR DISCOMFORT HOLDING YOU BACK?

Human brains are hardwired in primitive ways, with the main objective of survival: preventing the possible tiger attack, eating in abundance because food might later be scarce, and never burning more calories than absolutely necessary.

Primitive brains achieve the main goal of keeping us alive in just three ways: by prompting us to (1) stay safe, (2) seek pleasure, and (3) be efficient.

The humans whose brains did these tasks well survived and reproduced, and those of us living today are the recipients of primitive brains that are highly skilled at these three tasks.

When our brain is chattering the familiar messages of fear and scarcity, or prompting us to overeat, we can recognize that this is our primitive brain attempting to accomplish its main goal of keeping us alive.

If we were still living in a version 1.0 world with roaming tigers and scarce food sources, we could better appreciate our primitive brains. However, we live in a version 3.0 world (at least), and for us, it's a world that has been shattered.

In life after profound loss, our primitive brain is on high alert, functioning in protect-at-all-cost mode. Fear and scarcity are its main messages:

Don't leave the house.

Never go to unfamiliar places.

That person may be trying to help, but what are his real motivations?

Is it really safe for you to stay here?

There won't be enough money.

Can you do this life without him?

The brain prompts us to stay inside our bubble of familiarity. Is life easy inside that bubble? Of course not. But the brain craves what it already knows because it equates familiarity to safety.

So, although life after loss is extremely uncomfortable, the brain prefers the familiar discomfort over unfamiliar discomfort.

It's pretty terrible inside the bubble, sure, but outside the bubble is probably dangerous.

Luckily, other parts of the brain have different functions. The prefrontal cortex, unique to humans, is the part of the brain that can consider what's best in the long run, set goals, and help us achieve them. If the primitive brain is an unsupervised toddler running around with a steak knife, then the prefrontal cortex is the adult in the room. When we learn to activate it, it will calm the toddler, put the knife in a safe place, and counter the incessant, fearful chatter of the primitive brain.

We can think of the prefrontal cortex as our "higher brain." Using that part of the brain allows us to accomplish the following:

- Monitor our own thoughts and recognize that primitive brain chatter is an attempt to keep us alive.
- Notice that not all thoughts are true.

- Notice that not all thoughts are useful.
- Select other thoughts that are both true and useful and that serve us.
- Think thoughts on purpose.

When our world crumbles, the primitive brain takes the wheel. Yet it is never too late to activate the higher brain, the adult in the room. Ask yourself whether there is truth to what the primitive brain is suggesting. Then listen to your higher brain:

Your first lunch with a friend won't actually be harmful.

Going to that new hardware store is not actually dangerous.

You can do this.

Do the math, then decide if there is enough money.

An important waypoint in life after loss is to stop reacting to the constant chatter of the primitive brain and instead activate the higher brain's ability to think thoughts on purpose. That one step is critical to finding your way forward.

Chapter Summary

- Although life after loss is difficult, our primitive brains view this discomfort as familiar.
- The brain assumes that what is familiar is also safe, no matter how uncomfortable it is.
- The brain sees anything outside of normal as potentially dangerous.
- Therefore, the brain prefers familiar discomfort (safe) over unfamiliar discomfort (potential danger).

Application

In your journal, make a list of things you currently do that are familiar and feel safe. Now make a list of things you might like to do or try, big and small. Observe your primitive brain inserting its two cents, trying to keep you safe inside your familiar life. Next, imagine that you have no ability to feel fear and you are guaranteed safety. In this scenario, what would you do, try, and experience? Stretch your brain by listing at least twenty-five things.

19

SCARCITY OR ABUNDANCE?

In her book *The Soul of Money*, Lynne Twist suggests that scarcity is a mindset for most people, no matter if they are rich or poor. In our society, there is a prevalent sense of "never enough": not enough sleep, money, or time. We're not thin enough, smart enough, or pretty enough. There is lack of opportunity and lack of money. We don't get enough downtime for ourselves, or quality time with others, and we're always running behind.

How much more might this sense of scarcity be true for widowed people? For some, a significant source of household income dries up instantly and without warning. The responsibilities shared by two people suddenly need to be accomplished by one. Sleep is evasive, energy levels are microscopic, and the demands of the day are crushing.

After our loss, it slowly becomes clear how much we borrowed from our spouse. We borrowed confidence, support, our sense of security, and more. We made joint decisions and then had each other's back, and in doing so we shared responsibility for the outcome.

Our great loss is arguably the most profound example of scarcity. Without our person, we feel insufficient. In our minds, we don't have enough, and we ourselves are surely not enough. We are sure that we lack the knowledge, skills, and resources to climb the daunting mountain ahead of us.

Ironically, when we are at our weakest, we must learn to become our own source of confidence, support, and security. We must make decisions and then have our own backs and take full responsibility for the outcome. Once a happy and confident part of a two-person team, we must now learn that we, alone, are enough.

This growth starts with believing it is possible.

Beliefs are simply thoughts we think often. Thoughts are always optional, and thoughts ultimately create results in our life. Therefore, what we believe, we create more of.

Growth comes from noticing thoughts of scarcity as they occur and purposefully replacing them with thoughts of sufficiency—our own sufficiency and that of our resources. It's about learning to believe in abundance and learning to believe in ourselves.

If we believe in abundance, we create more abundance. If we believe in ourselves, we grow ourselves.

A scarcity mindset is fear-based and uncomfortable. A sufficiency mindset is unfamiliar and uncomfortable. So our options are two varieties of discomfort, each with very different results.

Chapter Summary

- Most people have a scarcity mindset.
- A scarcity mindset is especially common for those who have lost a spouse.
- When we are at our weakest, we must learn to lean on ourselves like never before.
- Scarcity or abundance starts with thoughts, and we can direct our brains to think thoughts on purpose.

Application

Do a thought download about scarcity. What, according to your brain, is not enough? Are you lacking confidence, know-how, time, money, wisdom, support, or understanding? Get it all on paper.

Next, ask yourself what else is true. What is abundant? What do you know? In what areas are you confident? What is your actual net worth? Looking back, what have you been able to learn and eventually master?

This week, pay close attention to the number of times your brain offers you scarcity-based thoughts. Acknowledge the normalcy of these thoughts, and then follow it up with some other true thoughts that are based in abundance.

20

WHY NEGATIVE IS NATURAL

You already know that our human brains are primitive in nature and that the brain's main objective is to keep us alive. Although today we are not likely to be attacked by a tiger, our hardwired brains are always on the lookout, constantly analyzing situations and quickly categorizing that which is safe or dangerous.

So, it's no surprise that brains are good at finding the negative. Back in the day, the brain had to quickly and efficiently determine whether there was a rock or a snake in the grass. Assuming it was a snake was the better, safer option.

People with brains that were most successful at spotting danger lived to reproduce, so now we are the proud owners of brains that have outstanding ability to spot anything negative, which could very likely mean danger.

Now add grief, and you've got a traumatized brain operating on overdrive, convinced that danger is everywhere, constantly seeking and readily finding the negative.

This tendency is called negativity bias, and it is nothing more than our primitive brains doing their best to keep us alive.

Luckily, we have other parts of the brain that are more in tune with modern life. The prefrontal cortex can recognize the primitive brain's focus on the negative, understand why it is happening, and then intentionally change the channel.

We can acknowledge the valiant efforts of the primitive brain and then demand equal airtime for what is right, what is working, what is positive.

Once we recognize our bias toward negativity and understand why we have it, we realize how much control we have over our mindset. We can separate the facts from the thoughts and remember that thoughts are not always true or useful, but they are always 100% optional.

So today, direct your brain to change the channel. What else is true? Where are there glimmers of goodness, even in this life after loss? If you ask your brain to look, it will find them.

Chapter Summary

- Quickly spotting the negative is akin to spotting danger.
- Spotting danger is the priority of our primitive brain, which is trying to keep us alive.
- Primitive brains dealing with grief operate on overdrive, searching for and finding negativity (potential danger) everywhere.
- Using our prefrontal cortex, we can change the channel and search for what is positive.

Application

In your journal, list all the areas of negativity you are noticing in your life. You will probably have a long list, and this is because your brain is doing its job of spotting what is negative (and therefore potentially dangerous).

Next, ask your brain to find areas that are good, positive, and hopeful. This list may be tougher to come up with, and that's okay.

Now, you are still entitled to your grief even if you have goodness, positivity, hope, and blessings in your life. This exercise is simply to help you (1) understand and appreciate your primitive brain and (2) activate your prefrontal cortex's ability change the channel so you can get the full gamut into your view.

21

OVERCOMING OVERWHELM

As if the loss of our person wasn't enough, widowed people instantly have double the responsibility, twice the tasks, all of the decisions, and often half the income. So it isn't surprising that one of the many feelings we experience in life after loss is overwhelm.

It's perfectly okay to feel any emotion, including overwhelm. It's also interesting to explore the emotion of overwhelm.

Like all feelings, a sense of overwhelm comes from our thoughts—for example, "There is so much to do," "I don't know how to do the tasks my spouse did," "I don't know how to make decisions on my own," "I am not sure how to make it on one income," and "I don't have any support." Consider the thoughts that cause you to feel overwhelmed.

It's both ironic and common that when we feel overwhelmed, we end up taking no useful action in the areas that need our attention. Overwhelm is a paralyzing emotion. As a result of inaction, we stay stuck in overwhelm, and we create more evidence that our thoughts are true. The things that need to be done multiply, and then we feel even more overwhelmed. It's a spiral.

The grief journey is an uncomfortable one (understatement of the year), and overwhelm is one of many uncomfortable emotions we will experience on this journey. But taking action in a brand new, unwelcome, difficult chapter of life is also uncomfortable. So ultimately, overwhelm tends to become our preferred version of uncomfortable.

But the tasks pile up: the bills need to be paid, decisions need to be made, paperwork needs to be done, the sink is clogged, and clutter is everywhere. Overwhelm isn't a useful emotion. What to do?

Examine the thoughts that are producing your feeling of overwhelm and ask yourself if they are both true and useful. Ask your brain to come up with alternate thoughts that serve you better and that produce a feeling other than overwhelm—one that will actually inspire action.

"I don't know how to do this" can become "I'm learning to do this." "There is so much to do" can become "I'm capable of doing a little bit each day." Those are examples, but it is important for your brain to come up with thoughts that feel true for you.

Try on each thought and ask yourself how it makes you feel. When you find the feeling that makes you want to take action, however small, ask your brain to practice that thought.

Because we are always in control of our thoughts, we can therefore generate any feeling we want to feel. Overcoming overwhelm allows us to take small action, which builds our confidence and belief in ourselves. Small actions taken over time create significant results.

Chapter Summary

- Overwhelm is a common and normal emotion, and like all emotions, it comes from thoughts.
- Often, feeling overwhelmed results in inaction, which produces even more overwhelm.
- Brains prefer the familiarity of overwhelm versus the unfamiliarity of taking action.

Application

Download the thoughts that create overwhelm for you. Get them all on paper. Notice the actions (or inactions) you take when you feel overwhelmed. Do you accomplish nothing at all? Ruminate about how much there is to do? Choose to do other tasks instead?

Notice the result that overwhelm creates in your life, and remember that all of it stems from the thoughts.

Next, try on alternate thoughts that are true for you and that do not produce overwhelm. Pause and see how each thought feels in your body. When you find a thought that feels true and produces a more useful emotion, you will naturally take useful action and start knocking tasks off of your list one at a time.

22

DECISION FATIGUE

For most people, one of the many perks of life before loss is making shared decisions: having a dialogue with your life partner, analyzing the pros and cons together, then making a mutual choice and ultimately sharing ownership of the outcome, for better or worse.

Relying on one another's strength, knowledge, and experience brings a level of comfort to the decision-making process. Generally, making mutual decisions means that you have each other's back, no matter the outcome.

Most widowed people have heard the adage, "Don't make any big decisions in the first year." There is some truth to that advice, but the actual experience of losing one's spouse means facing a relentless series of decisions. For some, the decisions start at the hospital, then the funeral home, and they seemingly never end.

After the first wave of decisions come many more. Sell the house? Clean his closet? Wear the wedding ring? Get an alarm system?

We must rely solely on ourselves to make these choices, precisely when we are at our very worst, and just when we need our spouse the most.

Enter decision fatigue—that exhausted feeling you get when faced with too many decisions.

Decision fatigue is draining on a good day, and in life after loss it zaps whatever energy is left. Our primitive brain is immersed in fear and scarcity, and from that place it suggests that there is always a right and a wrong decision and that decisions are irreversible, and urgent.

Yet often none of that is true. When you are feeling decision fatigue, ask yourself the following questions:

1. When must this decision be made?
2. What if there is no such thing as a wrong decision?
3. Is this decision reversible?
4. Are there more than just two options?
5. Are you making a decision from fear or faith?
6. Are you making a decision through a lens of scarcity or abundance?
7. What would it look like to make this decision and then have your own back?

In the spirit of never believing everything we think, we must learn to be "on to" our brains. We can become the editor of the thoughts our brains are offering us. When we make decisions when we are ready and when we have managed our mind, we can trust that there are no wrong decisions—there are only the decisions we make, which are right for us at the time.

Chapter Summary

- Often, the two people who are a married couple rely on one another to make joint decisions and then they share responsibility for the outcome.
- Widowed people are faced with a seemingly unending number of decisions to make.

- Decision fatigue is the weariness you feel when you are faced with too many decisions.
- Primitive brains suggest that all decisions are urgent, irreversible, and potentially wrong.
- When we manage our mind, we can trust that there are no wrong decisions, only those that are right for us at the time.

Application

Write down all of the decisions on your mind. For each, answer the questions listed in this chapter. Then, organize your decisions according to when they absolutely must be made. You can choose to believe that there are no wrong decisions. As you consider each one, make a list of pros and cons. Be sure you like your reasons for every decision you make. Decide, and then have your own back.

23

EMOTIONAL COURAGE

It's a natural instinct to avoid discomfort of any type, including uncomfortable feelings. In our society today, we tend to avoid difficult feelings. To avoid their feelings, some people overeat, some use alcohol or drugs, and others overspend their money or spend their lives overscheduled or constantly scrolling a social media feed. Each behavior is a Band-Aid, an avoidance strategy, a way to buffer our emotions, even without our awareness.

The question is whether these strategies really work, or whether they ultimately compound the problem. For example, feeling stressed prompts overeating, which may provide a short-term relief. But only moments later there is added guilt, regret, and feelings of failure, all of which prompt more overeating. Attempting to escape our emotions in this way ends up heaping more bad feelings on top of the original bad feelings, only reinforcing the desire to reach for that strategy of choice—a vicious cycle.

After my husband passed unexpectedly, as soon as I was able, I jumped headfirst into work. Work was like a vacation for my brain. It took a few years for me to realize that I couldn't outrun grief, and the more I ran, the bigger it became. It wasn't until I stopped running that I truly began to face it, feel it, and process it. I learned that healing requires feeling.

My widowed friend Sari once told me, "Teresa, grief makes you a better person." To which I replied, "Then where can I sign up to be a lesser person?" (It turns out there is no sign-up sheet.) She made a great point, though. Have you met a strong person with an easy past? I haven't.

What if instead of reaching for an avoidance strategy we were willing to feel the feelings? (See chapter 3.) What if we simply say, "I am feeling this way, and that's okay." That is emotional courage. Feelings are neither forever nor fatal. Sometimes we just have to be with our feelings, reminding ourselves that this too shall pass.

Before we turn to our avoidance strategy of choice, let's get curious about how we're feeling and whether overspending/overeating/overdrinking/overscheduling/insert-your-strategy-here is really the answer. Maybe instead we can just face those feelings head-on, sit with them a while, really notice them, describe them in detail, breathe into them, and wait for them to pass.

One of my favorite quotes by author Christina Rasmussen is, "You can do the impossible because you've been through the unthinkable."[1] Any difficult feeling I might experience today simply can't compare to walking through the early days of the darkness of loss. That thought gives me courage. I bet you can reflect on your toughest times and say the same for yourself.

Chapter Summary

- Avoiding difficult emotions is a common, natural instinct.
- We each have a different avoidance strategy, and often more than one.
- Each avoidance strategy has its own negative consequence, and the difficult feelings are always waiting patiently.
- Processing emotions instead of avoiding them is the best and most efficient way through grief. (See chapter 3.)

Application

Make a list of your preferred avoidance strategies, and then list the negative consequences of each. Examples include weight gain, poor health, wasted time, addiction, and so on.

Next time your brain urges you to reach for an avoidance strategy, ask yourself, "What feeling am I unwilling to feel right now?" Then spend just ninety seconds processing that feeling (see chapter 3) and notice if it loosens its grip on you.

Set a goal to spend ninety seconds every day processing a difficult emotion. As you feel stronger, increase this time to two minutes, then five, then ten. Your willingness to feel difficult emotions is your ticket to anything you could ever want in this life, including healing. You can do this.

---

1. Rasmussen, Christina (2013) Second Firsts: A Step-by-Step Guide to Life After Loss. Insights, Hay House

24

BRIDGES AND LADDERS TO NEW THINKING

Many of us who have lost a spouse have often thought that we will never make it through this darkness. We can't possibly imagine that the intense, soul-shattering pain will ever subside, that it won't always hurt like this. The darkness is so incredibly dark that we simply can't see any possibility.

Fellow widows often give helpful advice such as "Just breathe," and "Just get through this minute," and "I promise you the pain will change over time and become more bearable."

It's nice to have the support of people who are further along in the widowed journey. Their words can be a beacon of hope, and their survival is an example of what is possible.

I believe that if we have a pulse, we have a purpose. Over time, as we tend to our grief, process our emotions, and take lots of small steps, we can decide to slowly reconstruct our life. We can even decide to make the next chapter of our life (albeit one we never wanted) an incredible journey.

While the idea of starting an incredible journey might sound appealing, perhaps right now that thought is much too far away. That's completely understandable. Sometimes a bridge thought can help our minds open up to possibilities.

Here are a few examples of bridge thoughts. I've intentionally separated the first part of the sentence so that you can use it and fill in the rest of the sentence for yourself.

I'm seeking evidence that . . . my next chapter can be happy.

I'm learning that . . . my future can be a good one.

It's possible that . . . my life after loss can be meaningful.

I'm open to believing that . . . my future is filled with purpose.

I'm becoming a person who . . . believes in herself.

I'm considering that . . . I can live enough for the both of us.

While these may not be the right thoughts for you, perhaps some version of them might be worth trying on for size.

A close cousin of a bridge thought is a ladder thought. When you can't remotely believe that something is possible, simply choose to think that the very first, smallest step in that direction is possible.

For example, if you would someday like to lose fifty pounds yet you simply cannot fathom accomplishing it, you could try a ladder thought, such as, "I'm a person who can walk a little further today," or "I'm able to eat an extra serving of vegetables today."

As that smallest step becomes a habit, you can then think the next smallest step is possible; you'll soon begin gradually building rungs on the ladder toward your desired result.

Like all advice, if bridge and ladder thoughts don't work for you right now, simply leave them right where you found them and move on.

Chapter Summary

- Thoughts are optional, but we must choose thoughts that are true.
- Sometimes it's hard to believe that our goals are possible, which is when bridge and ladder thoughts come in handy.
- A bridge thought is a sentence with a toe-in-the-water beginning that states the goal at the end. For example, "I'm seeking evidence that . . . I can create a purposeful future for myself."
- A ladder thought is a sentence that contains only the first, smallest increment toward a bigger goal. For example, "I'm a person who can read three pages of nonfiction today."

Application

In your journal, try out some bridge thoughts by copying down the first half of a sentence listed in this chapter. Then fill in the second half with your own new thought. Choose to think the thought, decide if you believe it, and then notice how it makes you feel. If it generates a useful feeling, try it out for a few days and decide if you'd like to keep it.

Also experiment with ladder thoughts. Break down what might seem like an impossible goal into several steps and practice the thought that the first smallest step is possible.

You will use these bridge and ladder thoughts in the Belief Plan exercise at the end of this section.

25

IDENTITY CRISIS

Just a few weeks after the sudden loss of my husband, it occurred to me that my new best friends would be silence and solitude. I realized that I would need lots of both in order to figure out how to put one foot in front of the other.

It was only hours after this realization that my brother called. He was planning a trip to Disneyland with his wife and seven- and nine-year-old daughters and wanted me to go. Needless to say, Disneyland is the opposite of silence and solitude. But he was persistent, and against my better judgment, I went.

Somewhere between Main Street USA and Mickey's Toontown it hit me —I was completely lost. Not geographically, but in terms of not knowing who I was anymore.

Many widowed people struggle with identity. If I'm not one half of a couple, then who am I? For some, the loss of a spouse is just one of many identity-shifting events: an empty nest, a retirement or career transition, or the loss of other significant family members can all shatter our identity. For some, it all happens at once.

In the middle of a book, we turn a page and start the next chapter. Turning the page doesn't erase the story on previous pages; it simply allows the story to continue to shift and grow, building on the foundation of the previous pages.

Most widowed people would, in a heartbeat, go back to the previous chapter. Short of that, we refuse to turn the page. We argue with reality, wrestle with what is, rail against our circumstances, and end up exhausted.

We also have the choice, when we feel ready, to redirect that energy into turning the page, acknowledging a horrific life-altering plot twist, and then beginning to write. Because we have a pulse, we have a present and a future, and although the present isn't at all what we planned or hoped for, we can still decide to make the future incredibly good. We can decide that after enduring life's absolute worst, we deserve the very best.

My experience says that the more we move forward in honor of our spouse, the clearer we become about our identity in this life after loss. We find our identity in part because of our loss. We figure it out with millions of small daily decisions, through the familiar one-step-forward-two-steps-back shuffle of grief. We choose to believe that we are a person who is figuring it out.

In that moment at the "happiest place on earth," when I was profoundly sad, I simply decided that I was still my husband's wife and always would be, and that I would figure out the rest in time. I've done that, but I'm not finished because I still have a pulse. Truly, we can do the unimaginable because we have been through the inconceivable.

I'm writing my next chapter, and I hope you are too.

Chapter Summary

- Lacking a sense of identity is common and normal for those who are grieving the loss of a spouse.
- When you feel ready, it is possible to write your next chapter in a way that honors your late spouse.

- Identity can be found, in part, because of great loss.

Application

Identity often exists in the background of our lives, and it isn't until something changes that we start to question our identity or feel its absence. Consider your past and present identity. In your journal, write the following:

I was . . . What was your identity in the past? For example, you were a student, a professional, a spouse, a parent, part of a religious association, and so on.

I am . . . What is your current identity? Notice what identities from your past continue today.

I will be . . . What do you know about your future identity? For example, you will be a parent, a friend, or a sibling. You may have a spiritual identity, and perhaps you continue to identify as a spouse or your spouse's widow, and so on. Try to define your future self in terms of what you love (not what you will do). What matters to you? What brings peace to your heart?

26

THREE STEPS TO FINDING YOURSELF

Many people struggle to rebuild themselves after such a life-altering, profound loss. If we're not one half of a couple, then who are we? We find ourselves at a crossroad without a map and with our identity in question.

At such a critical juncture, our thoughts matter more than ever. Are the best years in the past? Is the future uncertain and filled with fear? Are you completely lost? Notice the thoughts your brain is offering you and remember that we should never believe everything we think.

Thoughts are powerful. And optional.

Thoughts are powerful because they create feelings, which prompt actions, which ultimately produce results, for better or worse. Our human brains often send us fearful thoughts, especially when a great loss brings our world to a screeching halt. This is simply a sign that the brain is doing its job—attempting to keep us safe during a time of major uncertainty.

But the good news is that we can direct our brain to choose any thought that feels true to us. Carefully selected, purposeful thoughts create feelings that serve us.

Most widowed people would do anything to go back to plan A. Short of that, we argue with reality, wrestle with what is, rail against our circumstances, and end up deeply exhausted.

We also have the choice, when we feel ready, to redirect that energy into picking up the pieces and starting to reconstruct ourselves. It all starts with our thoughts, which might be similar to these:

- I'm open to believing that I can rebuild my identity and my life.
- I'm seeking evidence that my next chapter can actually be a good one.
- I'm exploring how I can make myself a priority so I have more to give to others.
- I'm considering how I might live my best possible life after loss.
- I'm going to be an example of what is possible.

If those thoughts feel true to you, try them on for size, and see what feelings they generate. Or come up with other thoughts that are true for you that produce useful feelings.

Step one in rebuilding identity is managing your mind. To harness the power of your mind, select the thoughts that generate the feelings that prompt the actions that produce the results you want in your life.

Step two is making a list of things you enjoy, things you've been curious about, things you've always wanted to learn. Add in the activities that you're only recently starting to be curious about. If you gave yourself permission to be a beginner, what would you do? Include things you would like to try or explore. If it feels right for you, include experiences that you would like to have in honor of your spouse. As time goes on, you can always add and delete items from your list.

Step three is all about creating connection in the areas that are interesting to you. The loss of a spouse can sometimes mean the loss of social connections. So, redefining one's identity is a key opportunity to grow socially.

Alongside each item on your list, write the name of a friend or acquaintance who has similar passions and interests. This may be a great time to reach out and nurture your existing relationships.

You'll likely have blanks after some activities on your list, and that is perfectly okay. This is an opportunity to expand your social network in new areas that interest you. MeetUp, Eventbrite, uGetTogether and social media groups are good places to create new connections based on your blank spaces.

Making new connections with others who have lost a spouse or partner is easy thanks to the Soaring Spirits International Regional Social Groups and other events and programs. Grief Share is a faith-based opportunity to connect with those walking through the loss of a loved one. Groups are held across the country online and in person.

Expect that your brain may tell you that it is impossible to grow your connections during such a difficult time in your life. In truth, more than ever, social connections are happening virtually. Do what feels right to you, but don't let your brain get away with the thought "It's impossible."

By being "on to" the brain and choosing thoughts that serve us, we can start to believe that this next chapter can actually be bright. From that place, we can define ourselves based on our interests and passions, and then fill our lives with people who are like us. By committing to finding our authentic selves, we allow our new identity to reveal itself, and ultimately we can become all we were meant to be. Not in spite of our loss, but because of it.

Chapter Summary

Re-creating identity begins with three steps:

1. Selecting thoughts that are true and useful, and practicing those thoughts regularly
2. Creating a list of interests—past and present.
3. Forming new social connections around your list of interests.

Application

First, make a list of thoughts that your brain is currently offering you about your identity. Notice whether they are true. Note how each makes you feel, and from that feeling, what actions or inactions you take. Finally, what result are those actions or inactions creating in your life?

If you're not happy with the results, create a new list of thoughts that are true. See the examples listed earlier in this chapter. Notice how each makes you feel, and from that feeling, what actions or inactions you would naturally take. When you find useful thoughts, recite them regularly.

Next, proceed with steps two and three. Notice that your primitive brain will always do its job of keeping you alive. In this case, it will send you fearful thoughts about trying new things and meeting new people. For your primitive brain, what is unfamiliar might be dangerous. This is your chance to engage your higher brain to override the primitive brain. Be sure to engage with kindness—for example, "I hear you, primitive brain. I know you're trying to keep me safe. However, going to lunch is not dangerous. We can do this."

27

EXTREME EXHAUSTION

If we automatically received an owner's manual for profound loss, it would have an entire chapter on exhaustion. The chapter would not be about your garden-variety exhaustion; it would be about unprecedented, debilitating exhaustion, so deep and intense that every cell in the body is impacted.

Extreme exhaustion is the evil twin of grief. It moves into our lives and attaches itself so firmly to our entire being that we are sure we will never break free.

Keeping up with the day-to-day tasks is exhausting.

Taking a shower is exhausting.

The simple act of chewing food was, for me, exhausting.

At month five, I remember thinking that I'd never been so exhausted in my life. And that was only the beginning.

Profound loss is so life altering that we must draw deep breaths just to feel that we're not suffocating. We must will our heart to beat. Normally automatic bodily functions seem to come to a complete standstill.

Just existing is incredibly exhausting.

Exhaustion after loss is not something that a few good nights of sleep can fix—not that many widowed people are great sleepers, anyway. Insomnia is extra cruel when we're grieving and depleted, yet it is extremely common.

Our bodies are indeed physically exhausted from carrying the weight of our loss, from the lack of sleep and proper nutrition, and from the incredible stress of the situation.

Our traumatized brains are looping on our loss, trying to analyze it from every angle, determining what we could have done differently, searching the past for a similar situation to compare this to, and spinning in an effort to figure out what happened.

It's no wonder our car keys end up in the refrigerator.

Even deeper than the physical and mental exhaustion is the exhaustion that settles in our soul. We question our loss, wonder why we're still here, search for our new purpose in life, and try to find the reasons to keep going.

While there is no magic wand to erase exhaustion, the following five tips may provide some relief:

1. Judging your journey creates more exhaustion. Instead of thinking "Why am I still crying?" and "Shouldn't I be further along by now?" we can choose to think, "Okay, this is what we've got today," or "I'm doing this on my own timeline."
2. Guilt and regret are common emotions that add to exhaustion. When your brain offers you "proof" that you weren't a good enough spouse, remind yourself that you're human, you had no idea that time was short, and you have always done your best.
3. Avoiding the feelings that come with grief only postpones them and adds to the fatigue. Feelings wait patiently, and while they wait, they grow. Processing emotion is one of the superpowers within us that we can tap.

4. Be "on to" your brain and recognize that it is very likely operating out of fear.
5. Make self-care a priority. Figure out what brings a glimmer of peace to you and seek it out regularly with no regret.

Chapter Summary

- Exhaustion, common in grief, is due in part to insomnia but is also due to self-judgment, guilt, avoiding difficult feelings, and lack of self-care.

Application

Refer to the list of five tips in this chapter. For the first tip, make a list of judgmental thoughts that you notice your brain offering you. Notice how each thought makes you feel and act. Then, make a second list of useful thoughts that will serve you, noting how each makes you feel.

Repeat this for the second tip. Download your thoughts that cause feelings of regret and guilt. While these thoughts might feel true, in reality they are not facts—they are merely thoughts. Next, make a second list of alternative thoughts that produce more useful feelings.

28

ALONE BUT NOT LONELY

Here's a shocking truth: widowed people navigate the most difficult moments completely alone.

It isn't because people don't care. Often there are people in our lives who would drop anything for us.

It isn't because people don't try to help. The luckier among us have well-intended people at our beck and call.

It isn't because we don't have people we could call at 2:00 a.m. when the going gets tough. Many widowed people do.

Even in the best of circumstances—when we have people who care, who try to help, and who would answer the phone at all hours of the night—we feel alone. In less fortunate circumstances, it's far worse.

Those who love us desperately want us to be "better." To "move on." To get back to our "old selves." But the truth is that our old self only inhabits our former life. To many of us, "moving on" suggests leaving our loved ones forgotten in the past, and there simply is no such thing as "better," at least not on societal timelines.

Those who love us the most often don't understand that what they want for us simply can't be. They don't get it, and we wouldn't wish it to be any different. The only way to truly understand what we are going through is to walk in our shoes. So, if you don't get it, good for you.

Every time someone asks, "How are you?" we lie, and with every lie, we feel more alone. We are best actresses in a dramatic series. We don't "fake it until we make it." No, we show up and fake it and then go home and fall apart. Our need to be "okay" in order to make others comfortable is more evidence of our aloneness.

It's like having broken ribs: you look fine on the outside but ache with every breath.

Yet no matter your circumstances, you are not condemned to a life sentence of loneliness. The feeling of loneliness, like any feeling, comes from our thoughts. This is why you sometimes feel lonely in a crowd and why there were probably times that you felt lonely when you were with your spouse.

Might you be willing to believe that you don't have to feel lonely?

At this moment, there are many thousands of other widowed people seeking connection and understanding. If you are online, so is your widowed tribe. They are people who have their own version of the pain, people who unfortunately know the secret handshake, people who won't judge.

There are hundreds of social media groups for widowed people, and it's likely that at least one would be a fit for you. Most groups are private, so only fellow members can read what others post, and each person must prove that they are widowed in order to be added to the group. Group administrators work tirelessly to ensure that the group is a safe, welcoming, and supportive place.

While in-person interaction with people who understand the journey is ideal, social media groups are not limited to geography. They bring a sense of global community—hundreds of thousands of people who speak the language of loss are members. The groups inspire friendships and sometimes relationships and new chapters of life.

If social media groups aren't your thing, search MeetUp.com for groups that meet either virtually or in person. As I shared in chapter 26, making new connections with those who have lost a spouse or partner is easy thanks to Soaring Spirits International's Regional Social Groups, as well as Grief Share, a faith-based opportunity to connect with those walking through the loss of a loved one. In both organizations, groups are held across the country both virtually and in person.

Don't let your brain tell you that your loss means that you must be lonely. It's easier than ever to make new connections online. Now is a perfect time to find your tribe, feel understood, offer support and know that although you may be alone, you don't have to be lonely.

Chapter Summary

- Loneliness is a common and normal feeling in life after loss.
- Loneliness, like any other feeling, comes from a thought.
- The online world makes it easier than ever to create new social connections with people who understand the journey.

Application

In your journal, list the thoughts that create the feeling of loneliness for you. Notice which thoughts seem absolutely true, for example, "I miss conversations with my husband." A thought like this creates a feeling of loneliness for the one person you simply cannot have. It is best to process this feeling of loneliness (see chapter 3).

Perhaps you find other thoughts creating a feeling of loneliness, such as, "No one understands me." "I feel safer if I just stay home." "I really prefer solitude." These are thoughts worth examining if they make you feel unnecessarily lonely. Are these thoughts really true? What feelings and actions do they prompt, and do they lead to results you want for your life? If not, it's time to explore new thoughts that are both true and useful.

29

ENVY, WIDOWED STYLE

Envy is known as the art of counting another's blessings instead of your own. Like every other thing that changes with the loss of a spouse, we suddenly have new reasons to be envious.

Seeing an older couple walking hand in hand can be like a gut punch, right when you least expect it. That couple has exactly what we don't: the blessing of growing old together.

Like every other feeling, envy comes from our thoughts. We tell ourselves that the couple has been married more than fifty years. They promised forever and they're living it now, hand in hand, for better or worse. They got lucky, while we got cheated.

It can be tough to count our blessings when chief among them was ripped from our lives.

Thoughts like these create suffering that is piled on top of the pain that comes from losing our other half. As if the pain weren't enough.

What if that older couple were a widow and a widower who found each other late in life and courageously decided that their hearts were capable of even more love, that life could actually be beautiful again?

If that were true, envy quickly turns to inspiration. Even if it's not true, holding on to thoughts that lead to a feeling of envy robs us of our peace. Envy makes us even more miserable. It is a special kind of torture.

Our thoughts are always 100% optional. For every thought that our brains offer us, an infinite number of other thoughts are available and equally true. Since thoughts create feelings, we have the power to feel any feeling (as long as it's coming from a thought that we authentically believe).

Consequently, we need not suffer with envy. Not only because it feels rotten, but also because we can redirect our energy to processing the pain that comes with loss—which is time well spent.

Chapter Summary

- Envy, like any other feeling, comes from a thought.
- Envy feels terrible and is unnecessary suffering.
- Because thoughts are optional, we need not feel the extra suffering of envy.

Application

When are you most likely to feel envious? Perhaps it's when you're scrolling social media, at a gathering with many couples, or sitting in church solo. Know that it isn't this circumstance that creates envy for you; it is the thoughts that you have when you're in these situations.

Make a list of thoughts that create a feeling of envy for you.

Take a few minutes and notice how envy feels in your body. Where do you feel it? How does it make you react?

Decide if envy is a feeling you want to feel. If it's not, make a list of alternate thoughts that are true for you, and notice how each thought makes you feel. When your brain offers you thoughts that produce envy, practice your new thoughts intentionally.

30

HOW GRATITUDE CAN STALL HEALING

As a coach for widows, I often talk with people who are using gratitude against themselves. It sounds strange, right? Let me explain.

Most people are never taught that it's okay to feel difficult or negative emotions. In fact, as children we are often talked out of them: "Don't worry." "Don't feel sad." "Don't be nervous." Many people grow up thinking that it's not normal or acceptable to feel negatively, that life is somehow supposed to be a bowl of cherries at all times.

So, if difficult emotions are perceived as abnormal, then we certainly don't learn how to deal with them (see chapter 3).

Then the unthinkable happens. The seismic event of a lifetime shakes us to the core and levels everything that was once normal, predictable, and safe in our lives. Any negative emotion we've ever felt pales in comparison. Profound loss deals up an assortment of emotions that are perhaps best summarized as horrific.

Like never before, we reach for our buffer-of-choice to try to dull the pain, at least momentarily, and despite the consequences.

We also try to talk ourselves out of difficult emotions. This is where gratitude comes into play. We somehow think that if we have many other blessings we're not allowed to feel short-changed.

We don't want to wallow in our grief, so we shame ourselves into gratitude: "At least we had three decades together."

We count blessings instead of feel feelings. We fake it, thinking that eventually we will "make it."

Well-intended platitudes offer up gratitude as an antidote to grief: "At least you had so many years together."

We don't feel entitled to our feelings of loss, so we kick ourselves with gratitude.

Gratitude becomes a weapon that we use against ourselves.

While gratitude is generally a positive emotion, when used as a weapon, it stalls healing. When we force thoughts of gratitude, we sweep the pain of loss under the rug. By forcing ourselves to count blessings, we resist the difficult emotions. And what we resist, persists.

The most efficient way through grief is straight through. Facing your grief head-on means feeling the difficult emotions that come with the territory. When you process each feeling as it comes, you allow it to be there without reaching for a buffer. You name it, notice where in the body you feel it, breathe it in, and observe how it changes over time. Be courageous enough to be fully present with the feeling until it loosens its grip. Processing emotion is a simple, yet powerful skill.

Gratitude is a useful feeling, but not when we use it against ourselves. We can count millions of blessings and still feel robbed of what matters most. It's okay to have enjoyed three decades together but still mourn for the two more you had planned. It's also okay to have had the most picture-perfect marriage and grieve hard for what was supposed to be.

It's possible to be grateful and to feel incredible pain, all at once. One feeling does not negate the other.

Using gratitude against yourself will not expedite your healing. Processing your feelings will.

Chapter Summary

- Many people do not feel entitled to the pain of loss because they otherwise feel blessed.
- Gratitude can be a useful emotion, but not when it is used to negate difficult feelings.
- Processing difficult emotions is the most efficient way through the pain of loss.

Application

In your journal, note all the reasons why you are grateful. Also list all of the feelings you experience because of your loss. Take a few minutes and feel both the gratitude and the sadness, acknowledging that each emotion has a place in your life.

The simultaneous feeling of gratitude and sadness is just one example of the duality of life after loss, which is a place where seemingly contradictory feelings coexist in unprecedented ways. It can feel disorienting to experience such a range of emotions all at once, yet this is the authentic human experience of life after loss.

31

HE WOULD BE SO DISAPPOINTED IN ME

Understatement of the year: losing a spouse is hard. There is crushing pain that comes with the territory. We miss our partner's physical presence, mourn our shared past, and grieve for the future we had planned.

But the difficulty doesn't stop there. In addition to the pain that comes with loss is the extra-large serving of suffering that our brains inadvertently create.

Just one example of this suffering is fear, which can so easily become our mindset after loss. Our brains have been traumatized, so it makes sense that they kick into full-fledged "protect us from everything" mode. For me, fear dictated my every decision and most of my thoughts, but I could not identify it as fear. I just thought I was downing in grief.

Had I been able to identify the profound fear that was dictating my every move, I could have better understood my journey.

I could have been "on to" my brain. I could have said to myself, "Brain, I hear you and I know that you're trying to protect me, but we are safe." It's easy to let fear drive the car, so to speak, and yet the goal is that we drive the car (and allow fear to ride in the back seat).

Fearing that we are disappointing our husband is a special kind of torture. We tell ourselves that if we are "strong" we are succeeding and making him proud, and if we are "weak" then we're failing and disappointing him. These thoughts pile suffering on top of the pain, as if the pain weren't already enough.

The truth is that life after loss is a place of devastation that leaves us picking up a million pieces and trying to reassemble some form of a life. It's a messy, difficult process, and it's hard to see any result.

As we stand in that pile of wreckage, we judge our journey as right or wrong, too fast or too slow. We decide that sobbing means failing and stoicism means success.

Deciding that the way in which we are grieving is a disappointment to our husbands is simply a thought—a sentence in our brains. It's a painful thought, and the good news is that it is 100% optional.

Most of our husbands didn't know what it is like to lose a spouse and then try to reconstruct a life out of the wreckage. Or how it feels to suffocate under the weight of grief that is parked on the chest. Or what it's like to freefall into an abyss of uncertainty and confusion. Or how the long days turn into impossible, sleepless nights. Or how the cruel transition from "we" to "me" feels.

Like most of society, they simply didn't know. Good for them.

What our husbands may have said is that if anything should ever happen to them, they would want us to find happiness again. Perhaps they even encouraged us to find someone else. Or maybe this was never discussed at all. In any case, after they are gone, we think they are looking over us, shaking their heads in disappointment. Which makes us feel even more horrible.

Please don't believe everything you think. Like any thought, that thought is optional.

What if the opposite were true?

Might it also feel true that he is still by your side, cheering you on, and not in any way judging you? Perhaps he is applauding even the smallest accomplishment. Maybe he is proud of you for having the courage to keep stepping through a life that feels like it has ended, however uncoordinated and shaky your steps might be. What if he is celebrating that you have so far survived 100% of your most horrific days?

What else might be true for you?

Chapter Summary

- It's natural and common to judge our own grief process.
- Many believe that they are disappointing their late spouse by the way in which they are grieving.
- These thoughts add unnecessary suffering to our pain, and like all thoughts, they are 100% optional.

Application

Jot down any thoughts you may have had regarding disappointing your late spouse. Getting it all on paper can be helpful. Notice how each thought feels in your body.

Then, considering the alternate thoughts I offered in this chapter, make your own list of new thoughts. Pause and notice how each thought makes you feel. Decide which thoughts to keep and which to delete, and recite your new thoughts regularly. The repetition will train your brain to think this thought, not the thoughts that create extra, unnecessary suffering for you. After all, you've been through enough.

32

CELEBRATING WIDOW WINS

The primitive human brain is designed with the primary goal of keeping us safe from danger. So, it naturally focuses on the negative or on things that can potentially harm us. Although we hear good news, our brains instinctively fixate on the bad news. Although someone pays us a compliment, we automatically focus on what we dislike about ourselves.

Survival depends on our ability to spot that which is dangerous; therefore, our brains are hardwired to see the negative. It makes sense, then, that we don't readily focus on what is going right or celebrate our wins. Yet if ever there was a time to find the wins, it is in life after loss.

Losing a spouse is a catastrophic event that levels everything that was once familiar, safe, and dependable. As we stand in the wreckage and attempt to put some pieces back together, we are hard-pressed to appreciate any real progress.

In my work as a life coach, I often ask widowed people what is going right in their life. This is a good question to ask ourselves. Although our brains are hardwired for the negative, we can choose to give equal airtime to the opposite. Where are the wins?

I would offer that the following wins are worth celebrating:

- If you feel like you are suffocating under the weight of grief that is parked on your chest, but you draw the next breath anyway.
- If you know what it's like to freefall into an abyss of uncertainty and confusion, but you choose to have hope in the future.
- If your long days turn into impossible, sleepless nights, but you keep putting one foot in front of the other.
- If you know the cruelty of the transition from "we" to "me," but you keep searching for your new identity.
- If you show up to work exhausted and do your best anyway.
- If no one in your life understands your journey, but you love them anyway.
- If you have so far survived 100% of your worst days: horrific, cruel, torturous days that you wouldn't wish on anyone.

You are winning.

I see you.

I celebrate you.

In what other ways are you winning?

Chapter Summary

- Human brains are hardwired to spot danger, which makes them excellent at focusing on the negative.
- As we are naturally focusing on the negative, it can be difficult to spot what's going right, and we tend to never pause to notice or celebrate the wins.
- We can direct our brains to change the channel and search for the positive.
- Wins in life after loss look different, yet they are 100% worth noticing and celebrating.

Application

Consider the wins listed in this chapter and borrow the ones that fit for you. Then, continue to make a list of your hard-fought wins in this life after loss. Train your brain to seek out something positive each day, however small. Share your wins with the people who love you.

33

WHEN AND HOW TO DEAL WITH HIS THINGS

One of the many challenges of life after loss is dealing with our spouse's things. From clothing to vehicles, computers to keepsakes, and all the little things in between, the weight of it all can be crushing.

We tend to have some unwritten rule about when we should be finished with this often overwhelming task. As if the timing is some measure of whether we are grieving "properly."

Our brains often tell us that we need to make these decisions quickly so that we can feel that we are "on track" with some notion of how we should grieve.

Of course, some people must move to a new home immediately and therefore have no choice in the matter. In any case, it's important to be "on to" our brains.

When we are feeling the weight of his possessions, we have an opportunity to examine our thoughts. The thoughts your brain offers you can make you feel either pain and dread or inspired and intentional.

I remember the many thoughts going through my brain as I was first considering what to do with my late husband's possessions. When I thought, "I'm letting him go," I felt terrible, which prompted inaction. When I thought, "He would want this sweatshirt to keep someone warm this winter," I felt inspired to take action on his behalf.

When I thought, "He loved this truck," I felt like I would be failing him if I sold it. When I chose a different thought, "He wouldn't want it to be wasting away," I felt motivated to sell it to a friend who I knew would restore it to its original 1947 perfection.

The trick, when you're ready, is to "try on" various thoughts and decide how each makes you feel. Eventually you will find the thought that will make the process tolerable at minimum.

My husband passed in 2012. I have given away some clothing, but not all. My first effort was around the five-year mark when I boxed up some warm socks for the homeless. A few years later I donated more clothing to the local shelter. His kids eventually picked out some things that they treasure. Using his shirts, I had pillows made for his grandkids and I intend to have aprons made for his kids, thank you, Pinterest. (Also see Christmas tree ornament ideas.)

I still have an assortment of shirts and ball caps, most notably his Navy Seabees items that he wore proudly, many decades after a less-than-warm welcome home. For me, the process of dealing with my husband's possessions has been little-by-little. If there were a race for the slowest, I'm pretty sure I would win. And that's perfectly okay.

I don't judge myself, and anyone who has walked in my shoes doesn't judge me either. Anyone outside of that circle may have opinions, but those opinions simply aren't welcome. I get to decide my own way forward, and I decide without apology.

You get to decide your way forward, too. Dealing with his things serves as both a reminder not to believe everything we think and a reminder that thinking thoughts on purpose is our superpower.

Notice any all-or-nothing thoughts you may have. For example, we agonize about whether to wear our wedding rings, as if taking them off is an irreversible decision. Similarly, we think of dealing with his possessions as dealing with every single thing, but that doesn't have to be the case.

We can decide that there is no timeline: not for grief and not for sorting through his possessions. The amount of time that has passed before we decide to box up some things is no reflection on us, no measure of grief, and especially no indication of the depth of love for our spouse. Our brains often want to make it mean something, when truly, it does not.

Chapter Summary

- There is no such thing as an appropriate timeline for dealing with your spouse's possessions.
- When and how you deal with their possessions is not an indicator of how "well" you are grieving.
- Carefully chosen thoughts can help us deal with possessions when we are ready.

Application

When you think about dealing with your spouse's things, what thoughts and feelings come up for you? Make a list. It may help to start with the feelings and then ask yourself, Why do I feel this way? The answer will be your thoughts that are creating the feeling. Get it all on paper.

Next, list your family and friends who might treasure one of your spouse's possessions. Then make a list of your spouse's and your own favorite charities. Perhaps the charity has a thrift store. If not, you may decide to sell some things in order to make a cash donation.

My alma mater has a clothes closet for interview-style clothing. Students can select up to three complete outfits per semester at no cost to them. Because I knew my husband would have liked to help a young man look sharp for his interview, it was much easier for me to donate his suits.

If you need to sell your spouse's possessions and keep the money for your own needs, you might consider the thought that your spouse is still supporting you.

Finally, create a list of thoughts that would make you feel purposeful and intentional about dealing with your spouse's possessions. Be sure each thought is true for you. Practice your thoughts for as long as you would like and notice how each make you feel. You will know when you're ready.

34

THE MANUAL: PART 1

Think about the person who frustrates you the most. Wouldn't it be nice if they would just change? Life would be simpler, easier, and more peaceful if they would just correct their behavior, right?

Any time we are frustrated by another person, they are failing to meet our expectations of them.

We have expectations for all the people in our lives, in fact. My teacher, Brooke Castillo, calls this the Manual. It is a rule book we have created for how we expect a person to behave so that we can feel how we want to feel. Here are some examples of rules that might be in your Manual:

If only they would realize that I'm not "over it."

I can't believe it. She told me that it's time to "move on."

He should have never asked me out so soon after my husband's passing.

She should call me back when I call her.

They should have invited me to the party.

She should be supporting me.

They should know what I need.

Most often we don't actually tell people what's in our Manual for them; we just expect that they will know. While having expectations of other people is normal, it is actually the source of great pain because it makes our happiness dependent on the actions of another person. It robs us of our power. It gives other people power over us. It prompts us to try to control others so that we can feel better.

The truth is that adults have the freedom to behave however they choose. People who haven't lost a spouse don't understand the journey. Those who show up try to say the "right" things and sometimes they say the most unhelpful things. They don't know what our needs are. Some don't reach out in the spirit of giving us space, or for fear of saying the wrong thing. They don't realize that even though we don't actually want to go to the party, we want to be invited.

In fairness, we were once in their shoes, and we also didn't know what we didn't know.

And besides, once you know that thoughts create feelings, you know that your feelings are an inside job; they are dependent only on your own thoughts, not the actions of another.

If we throw away the Manuals we have for other people, these people can no longer disappoint us with their behavior. We can let them act exactly how they act. We can stop expecting them to understand what they can't possibly understand. We can stop holding them accountable for how we feel.

Chapter Summary

- We have a rule book of expectations for every person in our life. It's called the Manual.
- We don't tell people about our Manual, but we expect them to behave accordingly.
- If people behave according to our Manual for them, then we get to feel comfortable.

- Adults get to behave exactly however they behave.
- Other people's actions do not dictate our feelings; it's our thoughts about their actions that cause our feelings.

Application

Write the name of one person who you would like to change. In detail, write what you would like them to do. Write down why you want them to behave in this way. How would you get to feel if they did behave this way? What do you make it mean when they don't behave in this way? What would it be like if you simply let them behave exactly how they behave?

35

THE MANUAL: PART 2

In the previous chapter, I discussed the concept of the Manual, our rule book for how other people should behave, and how having a Manual makes our feelings dependent on the actions of others.

Now let's consider the opposite. Every person in our life has a Manual for us: how we should act, how we should grieve, what we should and should not say. Their Manual tells them that we should be further along in our journey, or that we have launched impulsively and foolishly into our next chapter. We should cry more or cry less. We should have it together by now or we have it too together, therefore we must not have loved him enough.

Given that everyone has a different Manual for us, it would be impossible to follow them all. You may not even try to. But consider which Manuals you do try your best to follow.

Trying to follow other people's Manuals is a form of people pleasing, which is an attempt, with the best of intentions, to control others. We believe that, if we follow their Manual, we are helping people to feel better, to worry about us less, to rest assured that we are okay. We think that our actions can directly control their feelings.

Which is just not true.

No matter our actions, other people get to think whatever they choose to think, which creates their feelings, which prompt their actions.

We can lose weight, and one person will think we're too thin while another will think we are looking healthier. We can go out on a date, and for every person who thinks that it's a good idea there will be another who thinks it is much too soon. We can break down in tears, and one person will think we should be "over it" by now and another will think that we should cry more often.

We can live our lives trying to follow lengthy and conflicting Manuals, or we can live our lives for ourselves.

We can decide what's good for us and then have our own backs.

We can recognize that we have absolutely no control over other people's feelings.

We can decide that we're not responsible for how much or little other people worry about us.

We can stop seeking approval and acceptance from outside of ourselves.

Because feelings come from thoughts, how we feel is an inside job. And how other people feel is their own inside job.

We learned from parents and teachers to seek approval from others, but now we're adults. We may have received acceptance and approval from our husbands, but now we're widowed. We have perhaps spent our lives "outsourcing" our feelings, but now it's time to bring this work in-house. It has always been an inside job, after all.

Chapter Summary

- The people in our lives have a rule book for how they think we should behave. It's called a Manual.
- When we try to act according to another person's Manual, we

are people pleasing, which is an attempt to control the person's feelings.
- In life after loss, it's important to not seek approval from outside of ourselves.
- How we feel comes from our thoughts; therefore, our feelings are an inside job.

Application

Are you a people pleaser? Write the names of the people who you attempt to please. For each person, write what you are trying to make them think and feel. Also, notice what feelings you will not have to feel if you are in people-pleasing mode.

Imagine how you would feel if you stepped away from people pleasing and instead focused on caring for yourself. How would you feel? What would you do differently? Who might you become?

36

BOUNDARIES: WHAT THEY REALLY ARE

The two previous chapters covered the two types of Manuals: the ones we have for people in our life, and the ones people have for us.

Both types of Manuals are created in an attempt to control people, for their own good, of course. But the truth is that no one can control anyone, and it's no fun to spend our life trying. It's pure frustration.

For our own mental well-being, we need to burn the Manuals and let all the adults in the world behave exactly how they behave. This doesn't mean we condone what they do, it just means that we release the reins of attempted control (because those reins simply don't work and never have).

But what about situations in which someone's behavior is affecting us negatively and boundaries are necessary?

First, let's define the term *boundary*, and let's start by describing what it is not:

A boundary is not an attempt to get someone to follow the Manual you have created for them (remember, we burned the Manuals). Said differently, a boundary is not an attempt to control someone.

A boundary is a violation of your physical or emotional space.

Here is how to set a healthy boundary:

1. First, get clear on what your boundaries are. Think back to a time that you felt a boundary was violated—when you experienced an invasion of your physical or emotional space (not a failed attempt at controlling someone).
2. To set a boundary is to make a clear request with a clear consequence. A boundary allows the adult person to have free will—for example, "If you choose to smoke in my car, I will drop you off because I don't allow smoking in my car." (Notice that it gives the person free will to smoke if they choose to.)
3. If someone crosses a boundary you have set, always follow through on the stated consequence. Be willing to feel the discomfort of following through. Otherwise, the boundary will not be taken seriously.

A healthy boundary basically says, "You get to act however you would like, but if you choose to do X, then I will do Y."

Burn the Manual. Then, if you still need to, set a healthy boundary and back it up with the promised action. Your life will become simpler, and in this life after loss, you deserve it.

Chapter Summary

- Once you understand that you can't control another person, you are in a good place to create a healthy boundary, should you need to.
- A boundary violation is an infringement on your physical or emotional space.

- A healthy boundary is, "You get to act however you would like, but if you choose to do X, then I will do Y."
- Always follow through on your promised action, no matter how uncomfortable it feels.

Application

Consider the people in your life who you would like to control (perhaps the people you wrote about in chapter 34.) Imagine that you burn your Manual for them and allow them to behave exactly how they behave. Now ask yourself if they are violating your physical or emotional space. If so, a boundary may be in order—think about what that boundary should be. Then consider the consequence you will create and whether you will be willing to follow through on it should there be a boundary violation. Create the boundary, communicate it clearly, and always follow through.

37

FEAR OF BEING JUDGED

Imagine that I said to you, "I hate your purple hair. It looks terrible on you." Assuming that your hair is any color except purple, you might wonder about my eyesight, but aside from that, you wouldn't give the comment a second thought. It would roll right off your back. You wouldn't ruminate about it, question whether I was right, or second guess your actual hair color.

On the other hand, if your hair color was purple, you might feel offended.

As people living in life after loss, we often fear being judged by others. We think thoughts like the following:

What will people say if I go out to dinner so soon?

I don't want others to see me laughing . . . they will think that I'm "over it" already.

What will they think of me if I go out on a date?

How will my kids react if I introduce them to someone I'm dating?

We also feel the sting of being judged by others when we hear comments such as these:

You're not dealing with this properly.

Aren't you over it by now?

You've got to let him go.

It's time to move on.

Why are you dating so soon?

You shouldn't be making such big decisions already.

We fear being judged and we feel hurt when we are judged only when we are in agreement with the person making the judgments—only when deep down, we are already judging ourselves.

We talk to friends about these sorts of interactions, and they commiserate with us, telling us how rude and insensitive the comment was. But their validation doesn't solve the hurt because the hurt is deeper. The problem isn't what another person said (or what they might say). The problem is what we are already thinking about ourselves:

The length of my misery is an indicator of the depth of my love for him.

If I laugh out loud, it would be disrespectful to him.

If I join a dating site, it would be dishonoring our marriage and negating our love.

Being afraid of being judged or feeling the sting of judgment presents an opportunity for us to examine our own thoughts—to consider that, deep down, we might be in agreement. And then we have the chance to remember that all thoughts are 100% optional. Thoughts that cause extra suffering do not serve us. Let's face it: the pain of our loss is plenty. The last thing we need is added suffering.

Examine your thoughts. Are they both true and useful? (Hint: If they make you feel horrible, they're very likely not useful.) If they are not both true and useful, it's time to choose other thoughts, on purpose, that are 100% true for you.

Chapter Summary

- We fear judgment from others in areas in which we are already judging ourselves.
- We feel the sting of judgment from others in areas in which we are already judging ourselves.
- Self-judgment is an opportunity to examine our thoughts and determine if they are both true and useful.

Application

In your journal, write the various ways in which you fear judgment from others. Also, write the ways in which you have felt the sting of judgment from others. Deep down, are you already judging yourself in these same areas?

In what ways are you judging yourself and your journey? Make a list. Notice how each thought makes you feel. Decide if each thought is true, and whether it is serving you. Commit to the thoughts that serve you well and will help you navigate your journey and become the next version of you.

38

A SIMPLE APPROACH TO REDUCING MENTAL CLUTTER

In life after loss, our brains are traumatized and shaken to the core. There is so much to try to understand, decisions to make, and details to sort out. Our brains will have us believe that we must decide on everything immediately, which causes overwhelm and results in deciding on nothing. Our brains also pose thousands of questions a day. Some of these may sound familiar to you:

Why did this happen?

Do I have enough money?

Why him and not some serial killer?

How do I fix the sink?

Can I survive this?

Do I want to survive without him?

Why him and not me?

Am I safe here without him?

Do I stay here or sell?

While being inundated with questions feels like drowning in a sea of unknown, it is actually our primitive brains doing their job. There was a time in which fast decision-making meant the difference between safety and danger, between surviving or not. The early humans with brains that were most nimble survived to reproduce. Those of us who are alive today are the recipients of well-honed primitive brains that are adept at keeping us safe.

Although we still have primitive brains functioning in protect-us-at-all-costs mode, we no longer live in a primitive world. We can appreciate our brains for doing their job, and then we can remember that we should not believe everything we think.

An important way to be "on to" our brains is to ask ourselves whether we really need to make the decisions or answer the questions immediately. After months of drowning in the many unknowns, I created three file folders in my brain. One was labeled, "I'll never understand in this life." Another was, "I need to figure this out eventually, but not immediately." And the third was, "I need to figure this out soon."

From then on, any unknown that my brain insisted I solve immediately was filed in the appropriate folder.

It was a great relief to use the "I'll never understand in this life" folder, and I used it often. Much less frequently did I expend my limited mental energy attempting to understand why this happened. I could redirect that energy and brainpower elsewhere.

Filing unknowns into the "I need to figure this out eventually, but not immediately" category also took a great deal of pressure off. It reduced the sense of urgency that my brain was offering me. My new thought was, *I'll get to it. Just not right now. And that's perfectly okay.*

Then, with those less-urgent unknowns filed away, I could direct my focus to the "I need to figure this out soon," category. I was able to tackle one thing at a time, ask for the help I needed, and eventually cross things off my list.

I learned that, when we are dealing with many questions at once, our brains will typically offer us two solutions: A or B. Black or white. Right or wrong. This response makes sense when we consider our primitive brains' desire to quickly categorize the world into safety or danger.

But the truth is that there are very likely a myriad of possible answers. Our growth happens when we learn to challenge the answer that seems the most true.

To summarize, when your brain presents an unknown that needs to be understood immediately, ask yourself these questions:

1. Is this really urgent (or even possible) to understand? File it in the appropriate folder.
2. If you need to figure it out soon, ask yourself if there are really only two options. Brainstorm all possibilities. Make a list of ten or more options.
3. Am I willing to be wrong about the option that seems the most correct? What if the opposite were true?

Don't stay in decision fatigue. List the reasons for the decision you have made and be sure you like your reasons. Decide and then have your own back. You've got this.

Chapter Summary

- In life after loss, the brain poses a myriad of questions.
- The primitive brain urges us to decide immediately, and to pick from one of two possible options.
- In reality, not all questions can be answered, and some do not need an immediate answer.
- Very often there are more than just two possible answers.

Application

Make a list of the various questions that your brain is posing. Getting them all on paper will be helpful. Review your list from a place of understanding, acknowledging that your brain is simply trying to do its job of protecting you.

Then, for each item, ask yourself the three questions listed in this chapter and document your response. Finally, focus only on the truly urgent items and take the next smallest steps toward accomplishing them.

39

CREATING CONFIDENCE

For many people, being a part of a couple is a source of self-confidence, which is defined as "a feeling of trust in one's abilities, qualities, and judgment." Perhaps your spouse believed in you, encouraged you, and reminded you of your own abilities. If so, you likely outsourced confidence to your spouse, because if he believed in you, then you had a license to believe in yourself too.

But if we take a closer look, we can see what was really happening.

Confidence, like any feeling, comes from our thoughts. If your confidence was once outsourced to your spouse, you were simply borrowing his confidence in you, which made it easier to think thoughts that created confidence for you.

For example, "He believes in me, and I trust his judgment, so I must be capable of doing this," is a thought that likely produces confidence.

And then our source of confidence passes, and we find ourselves in the depths of grief, disoriented and despondent, needing more than ever a sense of confidence to face this new life. Our situation feels like the most painful irony.

But here's the truth: Our spouse's physical absence does not revoke our license to believe in ourselves. Confidence can still come from our spouse. But there is more.

As we navigate this life after loss, generating confidence for yourself becomes a powerful, and needed, skill. Confidence comes from a place of believing and trusting that you can do anything you want to do and that although you might misstep or outright fail, you will simply keep showing up as the best version of yourself.

Confidence is a skill that you hone by directing your thinking, which means choosing thoughts that are true and that create a feeling of confidence.

We often want to wait for big results to give us confidence; however, it actually happens the other way around: the feeling of confidence prompts actions that produce results.

From a feeling of confidence, we take action even though there is fear. Or, as my teacher Brooke Castillo puts it, "Confidence with fear mixed in is courage."[1] Confidence is making decisions and then having your own back. It is a willingness to fail and then try again.

Confidence comes from a willingness to experience any emotion. What if you fail? You may feel embarrassed or humiliated. But given that you've already felt the depths of grief, embarrassment or humiliation pale in comparison.

Confidence will fuel your actions as you navigate profound loss, and confidence will lead you to a future that you love. It all starts with a thought.

Chapter Summary

- Many people outsource confidence to another person, often a spouse.
- In reality, confidence, like all feelings, comes from a thought.
- An important skill in life after loss is generating confidence

ourselves, by choosing thoughts that are true and create a feeling of confidence.

- From a feeling of confidence, we take action.

Application

If you are lacking the confidence you need to step through this life, be "on to" your brain. What thoughts are you currently thinking that are preventing you from feeling confident? Notice that these thoughts are not serving you.

Next, create a list of alternate thoughts that are true for you and create a feeling of confidence. What actions might you take from this feeling?

Write the story you currently tell about yourself, then write the story you want to tell about yourself.

---

1. https://thelifecoachschool.com/podcast/58/

40

WHY YOU CAN'T STOP HITTING THE "ESCAPE BUTTON"

In my work as a life coach, I've spoken to hundreds of widowed people, and every one of us has an "escape button" that is our go-to method for attempting to numb the pain. This makes perfect sense given, well, biology.

Our primitive brain's main goal is to keep us alive. It does this in just three ways: by prompting us to (1) stay safe, (2) seek pleasure, and (3) be efficient.

So given those three main tasks, is it any wonder that our brains can so easily convince us to stay home (safety) and eat cake (pleasure) on the regular (efficiency)?

The primitive part of our brain is still version 1.0. Yet we live in at least a version 3.0 world, and we're not yet even talking about grief.

In our version 3.0 world, life is a 50/50 mix of positive and negative emotions. Negative emotions come with the territory of being alive (and needless to say, life-after-loss presents a whole new level of negative emotions). It's perfectly normal to experience a wide range of negative emotions, from boredom to bummed out, from disappointed to distressed.

Yet our primitive brains equate negative, difficult, or uncomfortable emotions with potential danger. Seeking pleasure, after all, is one of the three ways that our brains attempt to keep us alive.

So rather than allow us to experience a negative emotion, primitive brains naturally urge us to find an escape button, whether by resisting the emotion, reacting to it, or avoiding it.

Resisting emotions is to push them away, sweep them under the rug, or try to will ourselves to feel differently. We attempt to fake it until we make it.

Reacting to emotions is to snap, fly off the handle, or stay in bed all day because we think that the emotions are too tough to bear.

Avoiding an emotion is to attempt to buffer it with some sort of numbing agent. Rather than feel the pain, the brain suggests rather convincingly that we should seek pleasure. "Escapes" can include excessively using social media, binging your favorite show, overeating, overdrinking, overspending, and turning to pornography. Yet these are false pleasures, because each has their own negative consequence.

The other problem with buffering is that negative feelings wait patiently. It simply isn't possible to successfully resist, react, or avoid such that our feelings go away permanently. So now we have the negative consequence of the false pleasure *and* the difficult emotion that is still waiting for—and demanding—our attention.

Now add grief to the mix—an unprecedented level of difficult emotions. Soul-shattering. Unthinkable. Horrific. And, our primitive brains would have us think, unbearable.

So when faced with grief our primitive brains shift into overdrive, demanding that we hit the escape-button-of-choice like never before. We go on the run. We avoid. We react. We resist. We hold on to hope that, if we can stay on the run long enough, time will heal. And we wonder exactly how much time it will take.

My escape-button-of-choice was to be busy. At the time of my husband's passing, I had a career that required significant travel. After work, I'd come home to ten acres of property that needed my attention, and then I'd catch the next outbound plane. I was on the run for years, filled with fear that the emotions would overtake me.

I recently spoke to a wonderful person who is quite new to her grief. After her husband passed, she stayed busy with work. Later she retired but kept busy with volunteer work and activities she enjoyed. It wasn't until the pandemic kept her home and removed her escape button that her feelings caught up with her. Her husband had passed nearly thirty years ago. She ran in fear for thirty years, and yet after all that time, those feelings were still waiting for her, demanding her attention.

Time does not heal.

There is no true escape from the difficult feelings that profound loss dumps on our lives.

There is no such thing as speed-grieving, but there is a more efficient way, which is to process difficult emotions (see chapter 3). Because reaching for an external solution to an internal problem simply does not work.

So, if you've felt like a failure with every pound gained, dollar spent, and episode binged, please recognize that you are actually not failing. In reality, your primitive brain is in overdrive, doing its job, keeping you alive in the best way it knows how, by seeking pleasure.

In the next chapter, I will share more about using the prefrontal cortex to override the primitive brain and allow urges.

Chapter Summary

- Primitive brains naturally urge us to numb the pain of loss. This is called buffering.
- Buffers, or numbing agents, include overeating, overdrinking, binge watching, and staying busy, among others.

- Buffers are known as false pleasures because they each have their own negative consequence.
- Difficult feelings wait patiently and eventually demand our attention. Time does not heal.

Application

What do you reach for when the going gets tough? Have you comforted yourself with food, indulged in alcohol, binged watched, or been busier than ever?

When you notice yourself reaching for your buffer of choice, ask yourself, "What feeling am I not willing to feel right now?" Identify the feeling, then ask yourself, "What am I thinking that is causing this feeling?"

Spend ninety seconds processing the feeling (see chapter 3), and then if you still want to reach for your buffer, go for it. Eventually you will be able to spend two minutes, then five minutes processing your feelings. By flexing your I'm-willing-to-feel-any-feeling muscle, you will no longer be on the run or depending on a buffer. Being willing to feel your feelings is your superpower and your ticket to the life you want for yourself.

41

THE BEST-KEPT SECRET TO ACHIEVING WHAT YOU WANT (ALLOWING URGES)

In the previous chapter, I explained why the primitive part of our brains naturally urge us to numb the pain of loss. Luckily, other parts of our brains have different agendas. The prefrontal cortex, sometimes called the "higher brain," houses impulse control, judgment, and decision-making.

Often, the primitive brain's urges fly in the face of the prefrontal cortex's agenda. So if you've ever overheard conflicting thoughts happening in your mind, you've probably witnessed your primitive brain having a disagreement with your prefrontal cortex. These two parts of the brain tend to not get along.

The argument might go something like this:

Primitive brain: *Just eat the cake. It's been a rough day; in fact, it's been a horrible week. Cake will help. Lots of cake.*

Prefrontal cortex: *Really, you decided you needed to lose some weight. Nothing fits. You're uncomfortable in your own body. Cake is the last thing you need.*

If the primitive brain is like a child, demanding cake immediately, then the prefrontal cortex is the adult in the room, knowing what's best and making that happen.

How do we deal with an unruly, demanding child? We let her have her say: cry, scream, and throw herself on the floor. But we don't react to her demands.

We can deal with a primitive brain with its urgent demands in a similar way: we simply let that urge be there. This is called allowing an urge. We are willing to feel the discomfort in that moment, and we don't react. We don't reach for the cake, alcohol, social media, TV show, and so on.

When you feel an urge to "hit your escape button," set a timer for two, five, or ten minutes and just be willing to feel the discomfort during that time. Chances are that the urge will lessen or even go away completely, just as, after not getting her way, the child picks herself up off the floor and moves on.

A visual cue can be very helpful as you learn to allow urges. Grab a vase and some pebbles, marbles, or small rocks. Every time you have an urge and you simply allow it to be there without reaching for the numbing agent, add a pebble to your vase. In doing so, you are flexing your I-can-feel-this-and-not-respond-to-it muscle.

A wonderful goal is to allow one hundred urges. If you give in from time to time, no worries, just pick up where you left off. By the time you allow one hundred urges, you will (1) have fewer urges and (2) be completely willing and able to allow them when they do come.

You have felt the intense pain of losing your spouse, and you have survived. The discomfort you will feel when allowing an urge pales in comparison. Allowing urges takes practice. Let it be an imperfect practice, and you will make your way there, one pebble at a time.

Chapter Summary

- The primitive brain urges us to numb the pain of loss with some sort of buffer.
- The prefrontal cortex, or higher brain, has the ability to respond to the urges of the primitive brain.
- Allowing an urge to be there and not responding to it is a powerful skill.

Application

Whenever you have an urge to reach for your buffer-of-choice, ask yourself what you are feeling in that moment. Be courageous enough to simply feel that feeling without reaching for the buffer. Allow the urge to be there without responding. Add a pebble to your vase for a visual count of how often you are able to allow urges. Aim for allowing one hundred urges.

42

BELIEF PLAN FOR THE PRESENT

In chapter 16 we learned that one reason we stay stuck in a mindset that is not serving us is that our brains are made for efficiency. The main goal of our primitive human brain is to keep us alive, and one way it accomplishes that goal is by being efficient. When it comes to our thoughts, efficiency equals redundancy.

This need for efficiency explains why our brains offer us the same thoughts, day in and day out. We tend to believe that everything we think is true, so most of our thoughts go unexamined.

Thoughts we think over and over again become beliefs, and in the spirit of efficiency, our brains file our beliefs in the subconscious. After all, it is inefficient to consciously rethink things that we already believe to be true.

However, we have learned the following:

- All thoughts are 100% optional.
- Thoughts are simply sentences in our minds.
- Our thoughts are sometimes not true.
- Our thoughts sometimes don't serve us.

In previous chapters, I recommend becoming a better observer of your own thoughts and then learning to question each one. The goal is to realize that you are not your thoughts and to eventually become a fierce editor of what your brain is offering you. Because unmonitored, unquestioned thoughts running on repeat can become a self-imposed prison sentence.

In a life that has suddenly and irreversibly spun out of control, thought management becomes our first opportunity to *regain* control. Although our brains might be offering one thought on repeat, a host of other thoughts are also true.

We have the ability to direct our brains to think the thoughts that are both true and useful. By directing our brains we unlock the handcuffs and step into new possibility.

Since our thoughts directly create our feelings, and since our thoughts are 100% optional, it is best to choose thoughts that don't make us feel horrible. After all, this life is tough enough (understatement of the year) without our brains manufacturing unnecessary additional suffering.

I encourage my clients to create a Belief Plan, and I hope you will create one for yourself. (In fact, I recommend that you create a belief plan for your past—see chapter 16—present, and future.)

A Belief Plan is a list of thoughts that are true for you and that serve you. The plan can also include thoughts that you want to believe but don't believe just yet. It does not include thoughts that you do not believe at all. No unicorns, no rainbows, just truth.

Here is an example of a Belief Plan about the present. (Note: Not all these thoughts will ring true for you or serve you, but feel free to use the ones that do.) I've included common thoughts that create suffering, along with a corresponding thought that a person might find equally true and—here's what's important—creates a more useful feeling. Finally, I've added a column for a 1–10 rating, where 10 indicates very strong belief.

This Belief Plan is just an example. I encourage you to create your own using this format. Glance back over your notes from the past few chapters' Application sections. Include thoughts you think regularly that feel terrible (and make a note of specifically how each thought makes you feel). Ask your brain to find another thought that is true and useful. Then ask yourself, What feeling does that thought create? Finally, rate how strongly you believe the new thoughts.

Common thought	Feeling it creates	New thought (must be true)	Feeling it creates	Belief rating (1–10)
I can't do this life without him.	*fear*	*I can do today / this hour / this minute.*	*capable*	8
Trying something new is scary.	*apprehensive*	*It's okay to be a beginner.*	*curious*	7
I won't have enough money.	*insecure*	*I will do the math and explore my options.*	*intentional*	10
My life is too hard.	*defeated*	*I can do hard things today.*	*capable*	9
The hard times were supposed to be behind us.	*sad*	*Hard times of the past prepared me for this.*	*resilient*	9
There's too much to do.	*overwhelmed*	*I can do one small thing today.*	*purposeful*	7
I don't know who I am anymore.	*uncertain*	*I'm becoming a different version of myself.*	*open*	7
I don't have a purpose now.	*confused*	*I'm open to new possibilities that feel purposeful to me now.*	*intrigued*	6
I can't make a decision.	*unsure*	*There is no such thing as a bad decision.*	*empowered*	8
I should be further along by now.	*frustrated*	*I am exactly where I should be.*	*present*	7
My best friend should know how to support me.	*disheartened*	*My best friend doesn't understand profound loss. Good for her.*	*accepting*	9

Chapter Summary

- Beliefs are thoughts that we have thought often.
- The brain files beliefs away in the subconscious, making beliefs a bit harder to find.
- A Belief Plan is a list of thoughts that are both true and useful.

Application

Create your own Belief Plan focusing on the present. (You will create a separate one for the future in chapter 56.) But creating your plan is not enough. You'll also need to recite it regularly and evolve it over time. Find a creative way to integrate reciting your Belief Plan into your daily routine.

LOOKING AHEAD

Previous sections have focused on the past and the present, and now it's time to consider the future. Now, if you just read that sentence and had at least ten roadblocks instantly appear in your brain, that's perfectly okay. This section will help you look ahead in unique ways, demolishing roadblock after roadblock as we go. It will help you make sense of moving forward and untangle the beliefs that are currently keeping you stuck.

A client of mine described it as standing in a doorway but unable to take the first step forward. She knew that she wanted to recreate her life, reinvent herself and figure out how to love her life again, but she had beliefs holding her back. We approached it one belief at a time and today she's living and loving her life again.

This section is not about getting over him, moving on, or letting him go (see chapters 13–14). In no way does looking ahead or moving forward disrespect or dishonor your spouse or your marriage. In fact, it can be quite the opposite. Your life can be lived in honor of your spouse. Let me show you how.

43

WHAT MOVING FORWARD DOESN'T MEAN

Depending on where you are in your widowed journey, you may be noticing some "firsts": the first time you laugh out loud, the first time in a long time that you actually feel good, the first time you smile, or the first pleasant day after a long string of dark days. Or, maybe it's the first time someone catches your eye or the first time you allow yourself to think about finding a new companion or relationship.

Those are among the many small steps in moving forward. Some steps are intentional, and some catch us by surprise. This is the courageous act of putting one foot in front of the other. It is engaging in the one-step-forward, sometimes two-steps-back, uncertain shuffle of grief.

During this stepping-forward process, the big question is this: What do you make it mean?

These first steps forward were some of the very things that made me feel ashamed. I was making them mean that I wasn't honoring my husband and our marriage, that the length of my misery was somehow a measure of the depth of my love, and that I was "moving on," leaving him in the past.

I was wrong about all of it.

I realized that the thoughts that made me miserable were worth reconsidering. Were they actually true? Were they useful to me? I mostly answered no to both of those questions. So, I came up with new thoughts that felt authentic and true for me. Even when my brain wanted to loop on the old beliefs, I directed it to think the new beliefs on purpose. Here are a few beliefs that are true and useful for me and that I live by today:

1. Moving forward is not the same as moving "on." Moving forward is simply turning to the next page in a book. It is not deleting all the previous chapters but, instead, building on them, honoring them, and continuing to grow because of them.
2. It's okay if I smile today. I deserve that.
3. It's okay if I have a good day. I'm worthy of that.
4. It's okay if I laugh out loud. My soul is, after all, tired of crying. This life is a mix of both.
5. It's okay if I allow my heart to expand its ability to love.
6. My journey through grief is no indication of my love for my husband.
7. I have finite energy, so I choose not to spend any on judging myself or my journey. I'll simply observe it with compassion and curiosity.

Profound loss is hard enough to experience without adding more suffering in the form of self-judgment. By eavesdropping on our thoughts and finding the ones that cause pain, we can decide for ourselves which are true and useful and then put our brains on the task of choosing those thoughts instead.

Chapter Summary

- Moving forward is a courageous act of putting one foot in front of the other.
- Moving forward is not the same as moving "on."
- Moving forward does not mean that we are leaving our spouse in the past or dishonoring our marriage.

- Observation without judgment is a mindset that will help us move forward.

Application

What does moving forward look like for you? What are the small and big steps? When you think about taking these steps, what thoughts does your brain offer you? How might it be possible to move forward in a way that honors your spouse and your marriage?

44

WHAT WILL PEOPLE THINK?

For many widowed people, one of the numerous unwanted consequences of their loss is the excess of attention it brings. Friends, family, and acquaintances watch carefully—and mostly lovingly—as our life after loss unfolds. Yet, realistically, we can also be a favorite source of gossip.

After we experience profound loss, our brain's main goal is to protect us, which kicks a fear-based mindset into overdrive. Add to that mindset the fear of being judged, and it's not hard to feel paralyzed, lost, and alone. We fear that people may be saying some of the following things about us:

She is acting like nothing ever happened.

Looks like she got over him quickly.

She's already out having lunch . . . with a man.

Shouldn't she be at home grieving?

Anytime we fear being judged by others, we are revealing an area in which we have judgment about ourselves. And anytime someone's judgment of us cuts like a knife, deep down, at some level, we are in agreement with them.

For example, if I told you that I really dislike your purple hair and that it looks terrible on you, you would look confused, wonder about my vision, and never give it another thought. Because clearly your hair is not purple. But if I said anything that you even remotely agree with, my words would sting. You could already be thinking some of these thoughts:

I must not be grieving "correctly."

The length of my misery is an indicator of the depth of my love for him.

If I feel happy, then I must be "over it."

How could I possibly have feelings for another man?

Fear of judgment, and actual judgment from others, feels horrible but invites us to take a closer look at ourselves, our beliefs, and our areas of self-judgment. It's an opportunity if we choose to see it as such.

When you are afraid to be judged, ask yourself how you are already judging yourself in this area.

When you are feeling hurt by judgment, dig deep and uncover the ways in which you are in agreement. Decide if these thoughts are both true and serving you. If they are not, remember that all thoughts are 100% optional. It's time to find alternate thoughts that are authentically true for you.

In our life before loss, many of us outsourced our confidence to our husband. If he approved of our decisions, then we felt confident and self-assured. Reconstructing our life after loss means being our own source of confidence. It means having our own backs. The more we love our decisions, the less we need others to love them.

Profound loss casts a dividing line in our lives that clearly marks the before and the after. In the after, everything changes. Many of these changes are horrific, but some of them can serve us. We get to make new rules. We can become fierce editors of who and what we allow in our lives. We can become a new version of ourselves who needs no approval.

And then we can learn to simply be us and let the world adjust accordingly.

Chapter Summary

- Anytime we fear being judged by others, it reveals an area in which we have judgment about ourselves.
- Self-judgment comes from our thoughts about ourselves, which is good news because thoughts are optional.

Application

In your journal, do a complete thought download about the areas in which you fear that people will judge you. Then, write about the ways you have already felt the sting of judgment by others.

In what ways are you in agreement?

List the various ways that you judge yourself. Notice if these are true and whether they serve you. If not, direct your brain to consider what else might be true.

45

"CHEATING ON" YOUR LATE SPOUSE

In my work as a coach for widowed people, I often hear the question, "Is it normal for me to feel like I'm cheating on him?"

Thinking that we are cheating on our late husbands is indeed a common thought, and it often prompts feelings of guilt and shame.

Just the thought of possibly, someday, wanting to find companionship is enough to send us into a guilt-ridden downward spiral. For some, the notion of cheating comes with the creation of an online dating profile or deliberating about wearing wedding rings. For others, thoughts of cheating come up the first time that someone expresses interest, or when well-intending friends offer to play Cupid.

I faced a mountain of confusion with my husband's sudden passing, then I dealt with more confusion as I was trying to figure out how to live my life again. Later, when someone caught my eye, I came upon another heap of uncertainty. How could this possibly be happening, I thought, when I signed up for life? When I said, "Until death do us part," I meant my death, not his. How could this possibly be happening when I had a beautiful, peaceful, loving marriage that was an example to others of what is possible? I was baffled.

My heart was dragging me forward, but my mind had a long way to go to catch up.

Finding companionship or a new relationship is a matter of choice. It isn't for everyone. If you feel that it is not for you, I encourage you to make an honest list of all your reasons. Then, be sure that you like your reasons. ("No one would want me at this age/weight/etc." is not a good reason.)

If you decide to be open to companionship in the future, take inventory of your thoughts. "I would be cheating on him" is a thought that will keep you from loving and being loved in this life after loss.

This may sound counterintuitive, but you can move forward in a way that honors your spouse, even as you date and perhaps someday marry. Every step of the way, you will need to find the thoughts that feel true to you because they will allow your journey to unfold.

My own thought is this: He loves me so much that he wants me to live this life I've been given, and live it fully, and love and be loved.

Our late husbands have our whole hearts. But when we find love again, our hearts gain new capacity to love, and our new person gets all of the new capacity. It's a bit like having a second child—the love for the first is not diminished in any way. Or like lighting a second candle—the flame on the first is not dimmed.

These are my beliefs. They feel true to me, and they make me feel encouraged and confident, grateful for what was and courageous in creating what is to come.

Chapter Summary

- Feeling as though we are cheating on our late spouse is both common and normal, and it comes from our thinking.
- It is possible to move forward in a way that honors your late spouse even if a new relationship is right for you.

- The heart gains new capacity for love, which does not diminish the love for our late spouse.

Application

Whether you are open to a future relationship or not, make a list of your reasons. Whatever decision you make, be sure that you like your reasons.

If adding even more love to your life is what feels right to you, search your current beliefs to see what (if anything) is holding you back. Ask yourself, "What if the opposite is true?" Challenge your beliefs by trying out new thinking and see how each thought makes you feel. Authentic new thoughts will create feelings that will inspire action.

46

DARE TO DREAM

Have you allowed yourself to dream again? To consider what this life after loss could actually look like for you? Not in terms of just existing, or settling for some form of "new normal" and assuming that this is as good as it could be, but have you thought about what the best possible version of this chapter of your life might be?

Allowing yourself to dream wouldn't mean that you're happy about how your love story turned out. It simply means that your life is exactly the way it is, that you have a pulse, and that you are still living this one life. It means that you can choose how you'll live it.

Living your best possible life after loss does not diminish your love for your spouse. In fact, it can be an expression of that love. You could decide to live for two—to live a big enough life for the both of you. And you can even decide to allow your heart to gain additional capacity to love again, if that's what you choose.

I remember a time when any thought about the future brought an onslaught of fear and panic. Much later, I realized that I have significant choice in creating my future, that I can create it with my husband—even for him—and that in doing so, I am moving toward him. Those were the beliefs I chose that allowed me to start thinking about my future. Of course, your beliefs may be different.

If you are ready to start thinking about the future, consider twenty-five things that you want for yourself. They could be objects or feelings—anything that comes to mind.

Next, consider things you might want to do. Some people honor their spouse by creating a bucket list of experiences that their spouse wanted to do, while others make a list all their own. Would you like to see Yosemite's grandeur or the depths of the Grand Canyon? Pick up a paint brush or sing in the choir?

What have you always been curious about, but life got in the way? What old hobbies could be dusted off?

Your brain might say, "I don't know." It can be challenging to learn to dream again. It requires courage to think about your future as a "me" instead of a "we." But ask your brain to take some guesses. Nothing is set in stone. Just dream. And then dream bigger.

"You can do the impossible because you've been through the unthinkable."[1] —Christina Rasmussen

Chapter Summary

- It is possible to dream again and still honor your spouse.
- Creating an ideal future begins with thoughts.
- Settling for a "new normal" or creating an incredible life (and anything in between) are available to you.

Application

Make a list of twenty-five things you want for yourself. How do you want to feel? What objects do you want to have? What people do you want in your life?

Next, make a list of things you want to do, learn, or experience. Allow yourself to dream big. Brainstorm without any judgment. Just write and keep writing.

Finally, notice what thoughts are coming up. Do you think that dreaming about the future means leaving your spouse in the past? If so, how might the opposite be true? How can you live your future in a way that honors your spouse?

---

1. Rasmussen, Christina (2013) Second Firsts: A Step-by-Step Guide to Life After Loss. Insights, Hay House

47

DEAR NEWLY WIDOWED SELF

In the early days of loss when my world went dark, I could have never imagined my future. Well-intended comments like "You have your whole life ahead of you" sent me into a panic, as that was precisely my biggest fear. I wasn't even sure how to get through the current moment.

Luckily, I had a few mentors who knew the journey, and I was grateful for their wisdom. How much more powerful would it have been, though, to get advice from a future version of myself.

Looking back, this is what I would have wanted my newly widowed, not-yet-forty-year-old self, to know:

Dear Teresa of September 2012,

1. Everything changes, most of which is terribly difficult. You've lost your shared past, your dreams for the future, and his physical presence now, right when you need him the most. It is horrific, and although you can't possibly believe this now, you will not always hurt like this. You will survive this.
2. Making immediate changes, out of survival, will help you. Stop

exposing yourself to people and situations that drain you. If there ever was a time to say no, this is it. Effective immediately, stop people pleasing. You've got nothing to give right now, and that's okay. This is when you change the rules and establish new expectations.

3. Accept help from others. Yes, you're more comfortable giving than receiving. But if there was ever a time to receive, it is now. Serving you is how people can show their love. It is how people can feel that in some small way, they are of help to you. Just let them.
4. Solitude and silence are your friends. Create a simpler, quieter world. Be outdoors as much as possible.
5. You have enough energy to last maybe a few milliseconds. If you spend it in judgment, it will be spent foolishly. Relinquish self-judgment and judging others. You need to spend that finite energy caring for yourself.
6. Notice your thoughts, and never believe everything you think. Your brain will offer you thoughts that are neither true nor useful. Beware. These thoughts will pile suffering on top of the pain. And the pain by itself already feels unbearable.
7. Society isn't grief savvy, and that's the understatement of the year. Allow the well-intended to not know how to help, to nervously search for the "right" words, and to offer extremely unhelpful platitudes. Be glad for them that they don't know (and see number 3). Find people who do know profound loss, and you will feel less lonely.
8. Sleep is what you'll need the most, yet it will be evasive for a very long time. Panic attacks happen while you're awake and asleep. You will find that deep breathing and a quick prayer will help.
9. Your brain is cluttered with confusion, which leaves you overwhelmed. Know that you will never understand some things in this life. Other things you will need to understand eventually, but not immediately. A few things need your attention soon. File your thoughts into those three categories

and then you can direct your attention where it is most needed.

10. You will experience an unprecedented feeling of tired in the very depths of your soul. This exhaustion is due in part to trying to be stronger than you actually feel. Do what you can to nurture your soul, and over time you will find rest.
11. You will be surprised to hear yourself laugh. Don't make it mean anything. It is not disrespectful. (See number 6.)
12. It's been said that experience is the most brutal of teachers. And indeed, you will learn such important lessons that you will emerge a different person. While you would give anything to go back to your former life, you will also like the person you'll become. Your life after loss will be one of your choosing, not something you settled for.

There is more, but this is a good start, dear one. Just keep drawing the next breath, just keep willing your heart to beat. You have a pulse, and there must be a reason why. Above all else, find your why.

Chapter Summary

- It's great to have grief-savvy friends and mentors, yet the best advice can come from your future self.

Application

Consider the future version of you. She's created an incredible life that honors her spouse, and in the process, she has found herself and strengthened her identity more than ever. As you let your imagination go, be as specific as possible: Who is your future self, and what is her life like? How does she feel? What has she accomplished? Who is in her life? What is important to her? What advice would she give you?

48

BUMPING INTO LIMITING BELIEFS

In chapter 18 we explored the concept of familiar discomfort, which suggests that while life after loss certainly isn't a bowl of cherries, at least it is familiar. For our primitive brain, anything outside of our current comfort zone is unfamiliar and therefore potentially dangerous, so it encourages us to stay within the familiar discomfort rather than risk the unfamiliar discomfort. All this is to say that our primitive brains are doing their job of trying to keep us alive.

Surviving the loss of a spouse is to first find a way to exist and learn to step through life as "me" instead of "we." Surviving also includes reconciling the past and navigating the present. This alone represents significant work and major personal growth.

Some people decide they want even more out of life after loss. They allow themselves to dream again. Although life is most certainly not what they had planned it to be, they choose to believe that it can still be incredibly good. They believe that having a pulse means having a purpose.

Some choose to seek a new relationship, while others opt for companionship or new friendships.

Some set out with a bucket list of adventures that honor their late spouse. Others decide to reinvent themselves like never before.

All of this progress requires stepping outside of our current comfort zone. We must choose to be uncomfortable, on purpose, because on the other side of discomfort is growth and the possibility of a really great life after loss.

When we start to think new thoughts about what might be possible for us, we tend to bump into limiting beliefs that we had yet to encounter when we were merely surviving. Offering us limiting beliefs is the brain's way of setting up guard rails to keep us on the road of familiarity, but that's a road we no longer want to travel. Those guard rails sound like the following:

I'm not the kind of person who . . .

I've never been successful before with . . .

I'm just not confident enough to . . .

I wouldn't know how to . . .

People my age shouldn't . . .

I'm too overweight / out of shape to . . .

I'm too old/wrinkled to . . .

I can't ______ because I've always been too ________.

Remember, beliefs are simply thoughts that we have thought often. Yet no matter how many times you've had the same thoughts, they're still nothing more than optional sentences in your mind. You might be convinced that they're true, but again, that's just your brain being efficient.

Bumping into limiting beliefs is a measure of progress, a sign that you're not merely surviving but ready to grow. It's something to be celebrated. But don't stop there.

Don't let unexamined thoughts/beliefs become roadblocks to your growth. When you bump into a limiting belief, question it thoroughly. What if the opposite is true? Put your brain to work seeking evidence to the contrary.

Remember, you are not your thoughts. You are the editor of your thoughts. You control your thoughts. Which means you're in control of your feelings, actions, and results. Ultimately, your thoughts create your future.

Chapter Summary

- The primitive brain urges us to stay in familiar territory (even if it's miserable) because outside of it is unfamiliar and therefore potentially dangerous.
- When we begin to think new thoughts about the future, we bump into limiting beliefs that we hadn't yet encountered while we were merely surviving. This is a sign of progress.
- Beliefs are simply thoughts we have thought often, and thoughts are simply sentences in our minds that may or may not be true, and may or may not be useful.
- Unexamined, unquestioned thoughts can prevent us from creating a good life.

Application

Imagine what is possible for you in life after loss. A move to a new place? A new career? A new relationship? Many new friends? A cabin at the lake? Being fit and strong and at a healthy body weight? Being an example of what is possible in life after loss?

Glance back at your notes from chapter 47 as you considered your future self. When you think about the possibilities for your future, what beliefs does your brain respond with? What "guard rails" does it throw up to keep you on your current road? Make a list. Then question each one of them, even though they may seem true at face value. What if the opposite were true? And how is the thought serving you? How will it impact your future?

49

FAILING FORWARD

Navigating life after profound loss can feel like one failure after another. One step forward and two steps back is a familiar shuffle. But what if failure was the path to finding your way forward?

As they learn to walk, babies fall often. Each fall could be called a failure, but actually it is by falling that babies learn how to balance. Notice that babies are undeterred by the thousands of times they fall, and adults never say, "That one isn't ever going to learn to walk." We never see a baby fall and consider it a failure.

Although most people acknowledge that more is learned from failure than from success, no one wants to fail. We are conditioned to avoid failure. In school, we strive for the A. Employees reach for the highest possible marks on the performance appraisal. Athletes compete for the win.

It takes courage to be a beginner. Most people are so fearful of failing that they refuse to try. They hide away in the familiar, no matter how miserable it is. When the fear of failure is paralyzing, we fail ahead of time.

When we do fail, we feel like a failure. We make it mean something about us: our worthiness, our capabilities, our intellect.

There is a big difference between failing and being a failure.

The most successful people are standing on the biggest piles of failure. In contrast, other people had one or two failures and threw in the towel.

"The fears we don't face become our limits" is a favorite quote of mine by Robin Sharma.[1]

What if failure were the ticket to growth? If so, then failure becomes the path to the goal, and we would be willing to fail forward toward the goal. Because if we fail, then we are taking action. We are putting ourselves out there. We are learning and revising our strategy because by failing, we gain valuable information that we would have otherwise not had.

The worst thing that can happen when we try something new is a feeling: disappointment, discouragement, maybe frustration. Yet we who have lost a spouse know much more difficult feelings than these.

Now may be the time to live bigger. To step outside of your comfort zone and take action. To fail forward toward the life you want to live. What do you have to lose?

Chapter Summary

- Most people dread failure and are so fearful of failing that they refuse to try.
- When we allow the fear of failure to paralyze us, we fail ahead of time.
- Failure is the currency to achieving whatever you want in this life.

Application

In what ways do you avoid failure? What things have you never tried because the fear of failure kept you stuck? In what areas of your life do you hold back so as to avoid failing?

If you tried something new and did indeed fail, what feelings would you feel?

Failing does not mean you are a failure; it is simply a chance to revise your strategy.

What if you chose this thought? What might you be willing to try?

---

1. www.robinsharma.com

50

ADDED CAPACITY FOR LOVE

In my work as a life coach, I often hear widowed people say, "I could never find love like ours again," or "I'll never meet someone else like him." I always wholeheartedly agree with these clients.

When two unique people come together to form a unique bond, that relationship truly is impossible to replicate. But what if replication was not the goal?

However you would describe your marriage—beautiful, loving, good, insert your descriptor here—consider that there are other varieties of beautiful, loving, and good. They are entirely different varieties but are no less beautiful, loving, or good.

Maybe you find beautiful, loving, or good from friendships, family, or grandchildren. Or perhaps you find them in a new companionship or relationship.

When we consider this possibility, we can find ourselves stranded at the intersection of guilt and shame. Our brains may offer us thoughts like these:

A new relationship would be disrespectful to him and our marriage.

It would be wrong to find happiness again.

It would mean that I didn't love him enough.

We must question our thoughts: Are they true and do they serve us?

Navigating life after loss is largely about choosing our thoughts wisely.

If you are a parent to more than one child, you would likely agree that your love for your second child did not detract from your love for your first.

Similarly, lighting a candle from another candle does not dim the first candle.

If someday your heart finds new love, its capacity for love will expand. Your late spouse still gets all the love you have now. Your new love would get 100% of the expanded capacity. Your heart will love bigger; your candle will burn brighter.

I'm not suggesting that you should or should not find new love. I am suggesting that you don't let unmonitored, potentially untrue, unhelpful thoughts rob you of the future that you want for yourself. I'm suggesting that you not believe everything you think. I'm suggesting that you monitor your thoughts and that you are willing to be wrong: to consider that the opposite might be true. I'm suggesting that you notice how your thoughts make you feel, and from that feeling, what actions you take. Notice the results you're getting in your life and know that results are a product of our thinking.

I wish you new capacity for love: for loving yourself and finding your way to loving your life again.

Chapter Summary

- Replicating our love for our spouse is not possible, but there are other varieties of love available to us in life after loss.
- Often the notion of finding a new companion or relationship

prompts thoughts that create guilt and shame. These thoughts must be questioned.

- Any kind of new love after loss is due to added capacity for love. New love does not diminish the love you have for your spouse.

Application

Get out your journal and contemplate the following: If you have considered finding a companion or new relationship, how did you feel? If you felt guilt or shame, what thoughts were you thinking?

During your life, in what ways has your heart gained capacity for love (e.g., with new babies, new friendships, etc.)? Notice that new love has not diminished the love you had for older children or friendships.

51

GENERATING ANY FEELING

Chapters 3–8 revealed the circumstance-thought-feeling-action-result model, along with the concept that life is (and is supposed to be) a mix of positive and negative emotions.

Now that we understand this model, we know that we are not a victim of our circumstances because whatever the circumstance, it is our thoughts that create feelings.

We also know that, technically, there are no "good days" and "bad days." Instead, there are thoughts that create difficult feelings and thoughts that create positive feelings.

Of course, this does not mean that we should feel only good feelings, all the time. The authentic human experience is to feel the range of emotions. When our spouse passes, we want to feel sad (among many other difficult emotions).

And sometimes we want to feel other emotions. Sometimes we need to feel useful emotions. For example, my clients often say, "I need to get motivated" when they want to accomplish a task or work out regularly or eat healthy foods.

If you know the thought-feeling-action-result model, you know that you can generate any feeling you want to feel. You must first find a thought that is 100% true for you and that produces the feeling you want to feel, prompts the actions you want to take, and ultimately creates the results you want in your life.

For example, say that you want to feel motivated to eat healthfully. You know the feeling you want to feel (motivated), and you know the action you want to take (eat healthy foods). Next, "try on" different thoughts and see which one makes you feel motivated:

I deserve to feel comfortable in my own body.

I sleep better when I eat healthfully.

I have more energy when I fuel my body with good foods.

I am choosing better short-term and long-term health when I choose healthy foods.

These thoughts make me feel motivated to reach for healthy fare. Maybe they do the same for you.

What feeling do you need to feel today? Perhaps it's confident or courageous, intentional or inspired, purposeful or peaceful, secure or steady, motivated or maybe hopeful. Each of these feelings are "at your fingertips" when you choose a thought that is true and that generates the particular feeling.

Chapter Summary

- The circumstance-thought-feeling-action-result (C-T-F-A-R) model is a simple way to organize all things in life, and it shows the power of our thoughts.
- Life is not (and is not supposed to be) all positive feelings, all the time. It is a mix of difficult and positive emotions.
- When you need to feel a useful feeling, simply use the C-T-F-A-R model. Find a thought that is true and generates the feeling you want to feel.

Application

In what area of your life do you *want to* want to, but don't actually want to? What feeling would you need to feel in order to do what you want to do? Use the C-T-F-A-R model. Think about the action you want to take. Then consider what feeling would prompt that action. Next, what thought would you have to be thinking in order to feel that feeling? Also, what result would the action create for you?

52

HOW TO CREATE ANY RESULT

The previous chapter showed you how to generate the feeling you need to feel in order to take any action. Now I want you to know that you can create any result in your life—including, and especially, in life after loss. We can literally use the circumstance-thought-feeling-action-result (C-T-F-A-R) model as a way to create the future.

Think about the model as a list of five lines, one for each part of the model: Circumstance, Thought, Feeling, Action, Result. Anything you want for yourself can go into the Result (R) line. Do you want to find your purpose? Hit your goal weight? Make decisions with confidence? Travel to Spain? Earn more than you ever have? You can put any desire in the R-line and then simply work backward to fill in the rest of the model.

For example, say you have a background in finance and you want to start a business to help widowed people get their finances in order.

Your model would start like this:

C

T

F

A

R—Start business

Now, we work upward: What actions would you need to take to get your result? Think of as many as you can. It may be that the first action is to research how to start a business in your city and state. Brainstorm the name of your company. Learn how to create a website. Have business cards printed. Learn how to advertise online. Join a local networking group or your local chamber of commerce. Write down all the things you would need to research and do in order to hang your shingle, so to speak.

Now, working up the model, what would you need to be feeling in order to take the actions we just listed? Perhaps you need to feel motivated, purposeful, or intentional.

Next, what thought would create the feeling that would prompt the actions you have listed? Here are some examples:

There are many widowed people who need my help.

I have just the background that newly widowed people need.

I can help people in this unique way because I understand the journey.

You've completed this process many times in your life, albeit without seeing it in the C-T-F-A-R format. If you have a college degree, for example, your result is your degree. Your actions included applying for college, paying tuition, attending classes, and studying for exams, to name a few. With each action, you were experiencing the feeling that prompted the action; perhaps you were feeling motivated, excited, or driven. Those feelings were caused by the thought you were thinking at the time.

The loss of a spouse is a seismic event that stops our world from turning. It draws a dividing line in our life, forever designating the before and the after. It shatters everything we once knew as safe, certain, and predictable. It forces "we" to become "me." It changes relationships, and most of all, it changes us.

The loss of a spouse does not, however, require us to never dream again.

Sure, for a while it feels impossible to dream again, maybe even for years. But not forever. I believe that if we have a pulse, we have a purpose. We are living this one life, and it is not a dress rehearsal. This is the real thing. We don't know how many days or years we have left, but we do have exactly 100% of whatever time is left, and in the grand scheme of things, our time is brief.

The result line is yours for the making. What do you want for yourself in this chapter of your one precious life?

Chapter Summary

- The C-T-F-A-R model can be used with a future focus to create any result you want for yourself.
- Simply insert any result you want to achieve in the Result line and work upward to fill in the rest of the model.
- Profound loss changes everything, but it does not prevent us from dreaming again.
- Life is short and precious.

Application

In your journal, write about what you want for yourself in this chapter of your life. Your brain may suggest that you don't know, which is a way to avoid the work of thinking new thoughts. Direct it to make a list of twenty-five things (that you don't already have) that you want for yourself.

As adults, we like to have evidence that it's possible to achieve the results we desire. In your journaling, you may get stuck because you have no evidence that reaching your goal is possible. Remember that results come last in the model. Results happen because of thoughts that produced feelings that prompted actions. So the evidence comes last. It all starts with a thought.

As you journal, ignore your lack of evidence and ask your brain to make a list. This list is not set in stone, of course, but this exercise will crack open a door that has long been closed. That is the goal. Dreaming big starts now.

53

IDENTITY CREATION

As we make our way through life, we gain new identities and release old ones. In some cases, our identity is established based on the phase of life we are in. We are first a daughter, then a student, eventually a wife, maybe a mom, perhaps an employee or business owner. There was a shift in identity when we got the degree, when we said, "I do," and when children came into the picture.

And with the loss of a spouse, we face the most unwanted and perhaps unexpected shift in identity: going from "we" to "me." Do you know who you are now, in this life after loss?

What does it mean to be you . . . now?

One way you can know that you're being yourself is that there's no restriction to how you show up in the world. You don't second guess yourself. There's no self-judgment or questioning. There is simply just being you—telling the truth to yourself and being truthful to others about who you really are. When you are truly being yourself, you care very little whether someone is going to like you or not.

Consider the people who you think really know you the most. What have you shown them that makes them know you the most? What have you shown them that you don't show other people?

Now, complete the following sentence: "This person really gets me because they know this about me _________." That is who you are. That is your authentic self.

Being authentically you also means embracing the less-than-ideal parts of you. These parts may include your age, your weight, your body shape, your regrets, and your failings. It also means embracing the version of you who was transferred three times before being disconnected and is now back at square one, on hold again.

In chapter 3 we considered that life is a 50/50 mix—good and bad, joyful and uncomfortable. The less-than-ideal parts of you make up one half of your 50/50. If you can see those parts without judgment, then you can fully embrace all of you. It is the authentic human experience.

Now let's look at the other half of your 50/50. Ask yourself what you most love and desire. What fills your bucket, so to speak? Consider whether these things are a part of your life now and, if not, whether you're willing to honor them by making them a priority in your life.

For some, meeting new people is essential in re-creating identity. It's a fresh chance at defining yourself with people who don't necessarily know your story. You get to be you without fielding any unwanted sympathy, preconceived notions, or potential judgment.

A pivotal point in my own journey was signing up for Krav Maga (the Israeli form of self-defense) and, in doing so, meeting a great group of people, none of whom knew my story. During the classes, I was able to take out my aggression, face my feelings, and meet people who didn't know me as a grieving widow. I was grieving and widowed, truth be told, but I didn't feel like it when I was inside the Krav school. What a wonderful and healthy step toward the next version of me.

Do you ever think about why you are the way you are? Why do you have certain people in your life? Why do you have the job you have? Why do you dress the way you dress? Why do you have the car you have? These attributes point to your identity now, which is not permanent.

You get to decide who you want to be in this world after your loss. But as you contemplate your identity, please remember this: While identity is not permanent, worthiness is. Worthiness can't ever change or increase, because you have always been 100% worthy. You are 100% worthy of anything you want in this world, including and especially whatever life you want to create for yourself now.

Chapter Summary

- The loss of a spouse often prompts the questioning of one's identity.
- Being authentically you means not second guessing, judging, or questioning. It is to simply show up as you are and care very little about what others think.
- Re-creating identity is to embrace the parts of you that you wish were different as well as the parts you love, and it is to accept all of your characteristics, values, and history as the most authentic human experience.

Application

Ask the people who know you best to describe you.

Consider your own personal 50/50. What do you love about yourself? What parts of you would you rather hide?

Spend some time thinking about why are you the way you are. Why do you have certain people in your life? Why do you have the job you have? Why do you dress the way you dress? Why do you have the car you have? This is your current identity.

Your future identity is a blank canvas. How do you want it to look?

54

MOVING FORWARD CONFIDENTLY

In chapter 39, we learned how to generate confidence for ourselves, but confidence is worth emphasizing again as we look to the future. When we take new and bigger strides, we tend to bump into limiting beliefs that had yet to reveal themselves when we were living smaller.

As adults, we think that we can feel self-confident only because of experience. First we want the proof, then we can be justified in feeling confident. But the opposite is true. First we must think a thought that generates confidence, then we take actions, then we get results. Confidence starts with a thought; the evidence/experience/result comes later.

As young people, we didn't expect experience to give us confidence. At age eighteen, for example, there was no evidence that it would be possible to get a college degree, land a great job, or find the perfect spouse. Confidence that any of those things might happen didn't come from past results—because there were no past results—it came from a thought that might have sounded something like, "I've never done it before, but I'll give it my best shot," or "I'm capable of figuring it out," or "I can do anything I put my mind to."

After the loss of a spouse, many people very naturally lack self-confidence. But the irony is that our great loss can be *the reason for* self-confidence—like never before.

Self-confidence is, in part, the willingness to feel any feeling. If you're willing to potentially feel embarrassed, rejected, or humiliated, then you're probably a confident person. You will very likely put yourself "out there" in ways that others won't. You might start a business or ask for the raise or apply for the corporate position or create a dating profile.

Because what's the worst thing that can happen? The answer is always *a feeling*. Yes, our brains come up with countless possible events that could unfold in our lives, but when you peel it back one more layer, you discover that it is actually all about how we will feel should those events actually occur.

So, what if you were willing to feel any difficult emotion?

You know how to process emotions (chapter 3). You know that negative emotions, like positive ones, don't last forever. You have known the darkest darkness, and you have survived. No emotion will ever compare to the loss of your spouse. If you can feel those horrific feelings, you can feel any feeling. Rejection, humiliation, and embarrassment are child's play.

Chapter Summary

- As adults we tend to look for evidence in order to feel confident, but the truth is that confidence is a feeling that comes from a thought. When we feel confident, we take actions that produce a result. So the result (evidence) comes later.
- Confidence is the willingness to feel any feeling.
- Most difficult feelings that may occur as we re-create the future will pale in comparison to the feelings of grief we have already experienced.

Application

Consider the following questions. You may want to write your thoughts about them in your journal.

How is the lack of self-confidence holding you back?

What would confidence do for you? How might it change your life?

In what areas do you look for evidence so that you can feel confident?

If you were willing to feel any feeling, what would you do? What would you create? What would you be willing to risk?

55

POST-TRAUMATIC GROWTH

In his book *Upside: The New Science of Post-Traumatic Growth*, author Jim Rendon describes "how a horrific event with permanent, life-altering consequences can transform a good life into a profoundly better and more meaningful one."[1]

Post-traumatic growth requires that a life-altering event occurred; however, one does not necessarily have to have suffered post-traumatic stress disorder in order to experience post-traumatic growth. Also, post-traumatic growth is just an option—it is not a requirement or a moral obligation to turn your pain into purpose.

Although information about post-traumatic growth rarely hits the airways, research dates back to the early 1980s. The earliest researchers studied prisoners of war and, this won't surprise you, widows. They studied what people had learned from their traumatic experiences and asked them what they wanted to pass along to others. Widows described how their husband's death had pushed them to discover how strong they could be.[2]

People who experience post-traumatic growth are found to have the following qualities:

1. Increased inner strength
2. An openness to new possibilities in life
3. Closer and often deeper relationships with friends and family
4. An enhanced appreciation for life
5. A stronger sense of spirituality

These outcomes are not *in spite of* the life altering event, but *because of* it.

As a reminder, post-traumatic growth is an option and not an obligation. There is no requirement to find your utmost strength and purpose in your life after loss.

It is, on the other hand, available to everyone. It is a choice, and it all starts with a thought.

Chapter Summary

- Post-traumatic growth is growth that occurs because of a traumatic, life-altering event.
- Post-traumatic growth is neither required nor a moral obligation.
- It is, however, available to all.

Application

In what ways have you changed for the better since your loss?

In your journal, write about what you have accomplished (see your notes from chapter 32), your newfound strengths, and your self-generated confidence. What did you leave in the past (people pleasing, not prioritizing your own needs, etc.)?

Revisit the five outcomes listed in this chapter. How many of them are true for you, and in what ways?

1. Rendon, Jim (2015) Upside: The New Science of Post-Traumatic Growth. Touchstone
2. Rendon, Jim (2015) Upside: The New Science of Post-Traumatic Growth. Touchstone

56

A BELIEF PLAN FOR THE FUTURE

If you read chapters 16 and/or 42, you've probably already written a Belief Plan for your past or present. Now we will apply the same concepts in those chapters to creating a future that you will actually love.

Remember, a Belief Plan is a list of thoughts that are true for you and that serve you. It can also include thoughts that you want to believe but don't believe quite yet. It does not include thoughts that you do not believe at all.

Following is an example of a Belief Plan about the future. (Note: Not all these thoughts will ring true for you or serve you, but feel free to use the ones that do.) We will stick to the same format as in previous chapters, with a list of common thoughts that create suffering, along with corresponding thoughts that you might find equally true and—here's what's important—create a more useful feeling. We'll also include a column for a 1–10 rating, where 10 indicates very strong belief.

This is just an example. I encourage you to create your own Belief Plan using this format. Glance back over your notes from the past few chapters' Application sections. Include your common thoughts that feel terrible (and make a note of specifically how each thought makes you feel). Ask your brain what else is true and useful. Then, jot down what feeling that thought creates. Finally, rate how strongly you believe the new thoughts.

Common thought	Feeling it creates	New thought (must be true)	Feeling it creates	Belief rating (1–10)
I am too old and wrinkled—no one will want me now.	*unworthy*	*I always look my best.*	*confident*	8
Trying something new is scary.	*afraid*	*Everyone is a beginner at some point.*	*willing*	7
I won't have enough money.	*uncertain*	*I can create as much money as I need.*	*abundant*	7
I am too overweight to be desirable.	*inadequate*	*I am desirable at any weight.*	*worthy*	8
I can't make a decision.	*insecure*	*I'm capable.*	*decisive*	9
I'm not confident enough.	*unsure*	*I've made it this far.*	*resilient*	9
I'm not smart enough.	*dumb*	*There isn't anything I can't learn if I put my mind to it.*	*intentional*	10
I don't have a purpose now.	*lost*	*I'm committed to finding my new purpose.*	*purposeful*	7
It's too late to start over now.	*indifferent*	*The only person who can decide that it's "too late" is me.*	*eager*	8

Chapter Summary

- Beliefs are thoughts that we have thought often.
- A Belief Plan is a list of thoughts that are both true and useful.

Application

Create your own Belief Plan focusing on the future. But, remember, creating it is not enough. You'll also need to recite it regularly and evolve it over time. Find a creative way to integrate reciting your Belief Plan into your daily routine.

SPECIAL OCCASIONS

If you dread getting an injection, you probably tense up in anticipation. The anticipation itself is uncomfortable and the tensing up makes it hurt even more.

The same can be true of anticipating special occasions in life after loss. Many of my clients dread upcoming events on the calendar – understandably so. Instead of wincing at the date on the calendar, we discuss expectations and make plans to navigate the day, leaving plenty of space to feel the array of feelings that make up the authentic human experience.

Refer to this section for any type of occasion that is approaching so that you can exchange anticipation and dread with solid expectations and planning.

57

PLANNING AND NAVIGATING BIRTHDAYS, HOLIDAYS, AND OTHER SPECIAL OCCASIONS

There is always a national or religious holiday, birthday, or otherwise special event just around the corner. These occasions can have many widowed people feeling dread, anticipation, or anxiety. Depending on the occasion, other people can have expectations of us, and we typically have expectations of ourselves. There are parties planned, traditions to be repeated, and perhaps gifts to be opened. And in the midst of it all, there's the grief, the deafening sound of his absence.

Creating a solid plan for navigating the special occasions is time well spent. Here are five planning tips that may help alleviate the dread and curb the uncertainty.

1. Have realistic expectations.

Special occasions of any type can be tough. In year one after our loss, we don't know what to expect. In year two and beyond, we expect ourselves to be "better" (and others do, too). My experience is that every special occasion carries memories and traditions, and this remains true year after year. As time goes on, we figure out what works best for us. My clients often ask me if it gets easier. My response is that it gets different over time and becomes something more manageable than in the early years.

Expect that there will be moments of happiness and sadness, that you may need time alone, and that you will do your best to navigate the moments as they come.

2. Make time to feel the feelings.

If you plan to gather with family or friends, also carve out time to feel the difficult feelings that you'll likely experience. This past Thanksgiving, my ninth Thanksgiving without my husband, I made time for a long walk. As I walked, I felt the feelings, I ached for what was, I honored the pain that comes with great loss. I let it be there, and I experienced it fully. Later when I was with a small group of family, I was more able to be present because I was not busy trying to sweep the emotions under the rug.

3. Be alert to people-pleasing habits.

If you are a people pleaser, you will very likely want to make everyone happy on special occasions. Well-intended family and friends want you to "feel better" or "move on," or at least look like you're having fun. If ever there was a time to put yourself on top of your priority list, it is now. Continually ask yourself, What do you need most? What is best for you?

4. Make decisions and like your reasons.

Widowed people can struggle with decision-making, and special occasions present yet another set of decisions to make: Will you attend in person? Spend the weekend? Host everyone at your house? Cook a full meal? Keeping in mind your needs from tip 3, make your decision. There are no right or wrong decisions—only the decisions you make. Then, make a list of all the reasons for your decision. The trick to decision-making is liking your reasons.

5. Have your own back.

When we are part of a couple, we typically have each other's backs, so becoming widowed means learning to have one's own back. By having realistic expectations, setting aside time to feel, and banishing people pleasing, you have set yourself up to make the right decision for you.

You are looking out for yourself and your needs, and you like your reasons. Now it's time to stand behind your decision, no matter what others think. Your decision isn't up for debate. "I've given it careful thought, and this is what feels right for me this year," is a sentence worth rehearsing.

Chapter Summary

- There is almost always a birthday, holiday, or other special occasion right around the corner, and making a plan for how to manage them is time well spent.
- By following the five tips listed in this chapter, you can navigate these days in the way that's best for you.

Application

Take a look at your calendar and make a list of the birthdays, holidays, or other occasions on the horizon. Walk through the five tips listed in this chapter for each event and create a plan that seems ideal for you this year.

Rehearse the sentence, "I've given it careful thought, and this is what feels right for me this year" (or something similar) in advance.

58

AN AUTHENTIC CHRISTMAS AFTER LOSS

As Christmas or another meaningful religious holiday rolls around, we who have experienced profound loss may feel anything but merry and bright. The dread and anticipation have been building for weeks and then the day finally arrives. No matter if this is year one or year ten, it is perfectly okay to not be okay.

My husband's birthday is Christmas Day (making him the best Christmas gift my mother-in-law ever received, she often says). So, in my early years of navigating life after loss, I dreaded Christmas Day that much more. If I could write a letter to my newly widowed self, to be opened on Christmas morning, this is what I would say:

Teresa,

The weeks of dread leading up to this day were far worse than this day will be.

With that said, this day won't be easy, but it will have moments of happiness, and even joy. Don't forget to experience what is good: the people who *are* present, the health of those you love, the joy on the faces of the little ones. Try not to rob yourself of these moments because you are mourning the past moments. Easier said than done, yes, but it's a good goal.

You've got only a microscopic amount of energy to get through this day. Use it wisely. Self-judgment will waste all of it quickly. Notice your thoughts and how often you use the word *should*. That word isn't useful on any day, but it's especially unhelpful today. Today will be a messy mix of emotions, and you will do your best to navigate them.

Make space to feel the difficult feelings: the ache, the sadness, the longing for what was. Attempting to sweep those feelings under the rug will only delay (and compound) them. Making space for them gives you a little more control over your day.

It's okay to not be okay. It's also okay if you *are* okay.

Pace yourself. You may be able to experience Christmas only in small doses. Take your own car to gatherings and park so that you're not blocked in by other cars. Quietly leave when you need to. Or excuse yourself and go for a walk.

Know that well-intentioned, non-widowed family and friends desperately want you to be "better" and even "over it." Try not to expect them to understand what they cannot possibly understand. Appreciate their good intentions and remember that, once upon a time, you didn't get it either.

One source of heartache is not buying him a gift. Consider what gift you *can* give him. A random act of kindness? A donation in his memory? Or, possibly, the best gift you can give him is the way in which you live your life after loss. Maybe eventually you create a life that is big enough for the two of you.

Instead of "*merry* Christmas," or "*happy* holidays," I wish you the most authentic human experience on this Christmas in your life after loss—the full range of emotions that we so readily feel, often all at once. The sadness and the joy. The heartache and the happy. Feel every bit of it today and believe with all your heart that the future is brighter than the present. It is, I promise.

Love,

Future Teresa

Chapter Summary

- It is okay to not be okay. It's also okay to be okay. Meaningful holidays bring a wide range of emotions.
- Make time to feel the difficult feelings. Be as present in the moments as you can possibly be.

Application

If you know of a widowed person whose journey you admire, ask them what they wish they knew as a new widow who is navigating the holidays.

Make a plan for your holiday season using the advice in this chapter.

59

THE NEW YEAR'S EVE THOUGHT THAT CHANGED EVERYTHING

For many living in life after great loss, the passing of time means added heartache. With each passing day, week, and month, it can feel like we are moving away from our beloved, leaving them in the past.

My first New Year's Eve without my husband was horrific. I would no longer be able to say that he even existed in the new year. It was crushing.

I'm leaving him in the past.

I'm going to forget him.

I'm "moving on" without him.

Thoughts like these piled huge heaps of suffering on top of already intense pain. It was many years later that I learned that my thoughts are always 100% optional.

Beliefs are simply thoughts that we have thought often. So, if thoughts are optional, so are our beliefs.

I personally believe that I will be reunited with my husband one day, when my time on earth is over. This belief is available to anyone, regardless of religious affiliation.

Given this belief, when my brain offers me those old familiar thoughts about the passing of time, I simply choose to think instead that I'm one day closer, one month closer, one year closer to being with him again. I believe that I have said my one and only goodbye-for-now and am one step closer to that forever hello.

That is a thought that I personally believe. It makes me feel stronger and closer. It reminds me that this is all temporary. It serves me.

Does believing this thought mean that I'm not living my life, dreaming big dreams, and creating a life that I love? Not at all. I can do all of those things while I'm moving closer to that forever hello. I can have both: a great life after loss and an eagerness to be with my husband again.

That's the thing about thoughts: they should be true, and they should serve us. I hope you will try on new thoughts that serve you, especially as you face each new year.

Chapter Summary

- With the passing of time, we can believe that we are moving away from our late spouse, or toward them.
- Choosing to think thoughts that are true and serve us is key to moving forward without additional, unnecessary suffering.

Application

As the calendar turns to a new month or a new year, what thoughts does your brain offer you? In your journal, make a list of your thoughts. Note how each makes you feel and complete the C-T-F-A-R model accordingly. (See chapter 53 for more information on the model.)

If you don't like your result, brainstorm alternate thoughts that are true for you. Choose one and plug it into the C-T-F-A-R model.

Direct your brain to think true thoughts, on purpose, that serve you. Do this as you approach a new year and every other day of the year.

60

ANNIVERSARIES

The calendar is a keeper of memories, which means that in life after loss, dates on the calendar can pack a punch. It could be a wedding anniversary or the anniversary of meeting for the first time, or the first date, or the day you were engaged. Or it could be the often-dreaded anniversary of the death of your spouse.

Religious and national holidays are shared by everyone. But anniversaries are unique to you as a couple, which can make them more personal and potentially lonelier.

Anniversaries can lead us down memory lane, for better or worse, and they may happen one after another. It can feel as though we're constantly being battered by the calendar.

But if we take a closer look at anniversaries through the lens of coaching, we can view them from a different perspective.

The date on the calendar is a fact, or circumstance. As we learned in chapter 5, facts are different than thoughts. The fact is the date on the calendar. We have a thought about the date on the calendar, and that thought produces a feeling.

The date on the calendar does not directly make us feel any feeling. It is our thought *about* the date on the calendar that produces a feeling.

Thoughts are simply the sentences in our minds. They are what our brain is currently offering us. Thoughts are always 100% optional. They may or may not be true, and they may or may not serve us, so thoughts always need to be examined.

We can think thoughts on purpose as long as they are true. In doing so, we can generate any feeling we want to feel.

Does that mean that we should think only happy thoughts on anniversaries? Not necessarily.

We know from chapter 3 that life is a mix of negative and positive emotions. The most authentic human experience is to feel the wide range of emotions. Anniversaries often prompt lots of thoughts that bring out the gamut of emotions, all at once. It feels like some sort of emotional whiplash.

Here are five tips to navigate anniversaries:

1. In the weeks leading up to the date, notice whether you feel dread, anticipation, or anxiety. These feelings, like all feelings, come from thoughts. So, go to the source: What thoughts are causing these feelings? And are those thoughts useful?
2. On the anniversary, monitor your thoughts by journaling and note how each thought makes you feel. Remember that thoughts are optional and decide which thoughts you want to keep or delete.
3. Be willing to allow and fully experience the mix of difficult and positive emotions. Process your feelings using the steps outlined in chapter 3.
4. Plan to take good care of yourself. What would be good for your soul? Go do that or at least get it on the schedule.
5. Honor the day in some way, whether through a random act of kindness or a donation in his name to his favorite charity.

It takes a few years to know how to navigate anniversaries with confidence. It's trial and error at first, and that's perfectly okay. You may want to have plans A and B. My boss was kind enough to allow me to decide at the last minute whether I wanted to work or not on the first anniversary of my husband's passing. I opted for plan B, which was a hike in the mountains, and it was there that I found unexpected peace.

Now with nearly a decade of anniversaries under my belt, I head for the mountains with my dog Holly. I visit the lot on the little pond that we purchased with plans to build a cabin. I allow myself to think lots of thoughts and feel lots of feelings. I smile and I cry. I'm grateful for what was, and I ache for what isn't. I feel all of it, because feelings need to be felt on anniversaries and other days. It is the most authentic experience, and I allow every bit of it.

Chapter Summary

- Anniversaries are often dreaded and can be difficult. But it's not the date on the calendar that is difficult, it is the thoughts that come because of the date. Thoughts produce feelings.
- To be authentically human is to experience a wide range of emotions, from difficult to joyful.
- Following the five tips listed in this chapter can help you navigate anniversaries in the best way possible. Give yourself time to figure out what is right for you.

Application

As an anniversary approaches, if you feel a sense of dread, anxiety, or anticipation, journal your thoughts. Notice the specific thoughts that are causing these feelings. Ask yourself if they are true and whether they are serving you.

Consider the five tips listed in this chapter as you plan to navigate the day. At the end of the day, make notes about what worked well and what you will change for next year.

EPILOGUE

I recently noticed a question posed in a social media group for widowed people. The person asked if anyone else wondered why life had been so incredibly difficult. Scores of responses poured in with unanimous commiserating on the subject.

I couldn't have felt more different.

If I made my husband's life better, if I made him know the deepest love, and if, because of me, he experienced the greatest joys, then I would sign up again and again, with eyes wide open, knowing what the outcome will be. All day, every day I say yes to my life exactly as it has been and exactly as it will be in the future.

I don't wonder why my life has been difficult. I know that my life made my husband's life better. And I hope that my life helps to make the journey a little easier and less lonely for other widowed people. I could never do that unless I knew firsthand the darkest darkness. That's the life I have, and it's the one I would choose again and again.

I sincerely hope that my life lends you a candle in your darkness.

RESOURCES

The Sudden Widow Coach, www.thesuddenwidowcoach.com offers ongoing tools and resources for those who have lost a spouse or partner.

Soaring Spirits International, www.soaringspirits.org, offers a wide variety of programs for those who have lost a spouse/partner.

Soaring Spirits International's Resilience Center is a partnership between Soaring Spirits International and Schreiner University to increase the body of research on the loss of a spouse/partner: www.widowedresilience.org. The Widowed Resilience Scale is a useful tool for many people: https://widowedresilience.org/research/take-the-assessment/

Grief Share, www.griefshare.org, is a Christian-based support group for those grieving a loss.

Compassionate Friends, www.compassionatefriends.org, offers support for those who have lost a child of any age.

SOURCES CITED

[i] http://www.ipsnews.net/2020/02/widowhood-stressful-unprepared/

[ii] https://www.mayaangelou.com/

[iii] https://www.jonathanlockwoodhuie.com/quotes/inspirational/

[iv] Lewis, C. S. (1968). A grief observed. London: Faber & Faber.

[v] Rasmussen, Christina (2013) Second Firsts: A Step-by-Step Guide to Life After Loss. Insights, Hay House

[vi] https://thelifecoachschool.com/podcast/58/

[vii] Rasmussen, Christina (2013) Second Firsts: A Step-by-Step Guide to Life After Loss. Insights, Hay House

[viii] www.robinsharma.com

[ix] Rendon, Jim (2015) Upside: The New Science of Post-Traumatic Growth. Touchstone

[x] Rendon, Jim (2015) Upside: The New Science of Post-Traumatic Growth. Touchstone

CPSIA information can be obtained
at www.ICGtesting.com
Printed in the USA
BVHW030258141122
651880BV00016B/364

9 780578 311548